Special Needs in the Early Years

Special Needs in the Early Years

Collaboration, Communication and Coordination

Sue Roffey

David Fulton Publishers
London

David Fulton Publishers Ltd,
Ormond House, 26–27 Boswell Street, London WC1N 3JD

First published in Great Britain by David Fulton Publishers 1999
Reprinted 2000

British Library Cataloguing in Publication Data
A catalogue record for this book is available from the British Library

ISBN 1–85346–604–2

Typeset by FSH Print & Production Ltd, London
Printed in Great Britain by The Cromwell Press Ltd, Trowbridge, Wilts.

Contents

Preface

Ideally, services for children with special needs and their families would be provided as a result of joint planning at every level. We are still some way from this, and it is acknowledged that families often do receive a fragmented service. There is currently a determination from many quarters, including the government, to improve service delivery. The good collaborative practice for children and families which happens in some areas needs to develop nation-wide and be taken on board at the most senior levels of management.

There are many hurdles implicit in this aim and, although these issues are discussed, the main focus here is the promotion of effective communication and collaboration which helps to ensure that a child's needs are met in early years settings, particularly in partnership with parents. There is a focus on inclusion and the needs of teachers and nursery officers in mainstream provision who may be less experienced in working with young children with special educational needs and their parents. This book is intended to be a resource that will:

- clarify the contexts in which people are working
- clarify the roles that different professionals may have
- raise issues related to communication with parents and others
- provide a framework for joint planning
- explore ways of strengthening in-school communication and collaboration
- give examples of good practice which might be replicated or adapted.

This book covers the range and continuum of special educational needs, from those that are complex and require substantive intervention throughout a child's early years and education to those which are mild or temporary. 'Early years' within the context of this book follows the Children Act 1989 definition, which is from birth to eight years (DOH 1991).

Special Note: The use of the pronouns 'he' and 'she' for children are used in alternative chapters, with the exception of Chapter 5 which alternates throughout. The definition of 'parent' includes all those who have a legal or practical responsibility for the child's care and welfare. Where teachers are mentioned this also refers to any professional working within a nursery, other pre-school setting or infant school. Similarly, 'school' or 'nursery' refers to all early years educational provision.

Sue Roffey
London
February, 1999

Acknowledgements

Many people gave generously of their time by talking with me, providing guidance on specific issues, directing me to sources of information or reading drafts of the manuscript. Some parents of young children with special educational needs also shared their experiences with me. I am grateful to the following:

Joan Armstrong, Mog Ball, Cyndy Bowles, Lorraine Clarke, Kairen Cullen, Sarah Dean, Roy Earnshaw, Jane Elias, Shelley Flain, Elizabeth Gillies, Maria Greenwood, Julian Grenier, Ed Hook, Helen Horton, Margaret Hollinghurst, Colin King, Jane Knowles, Michele Lindsay, Karen Majors, Melian Mansfield, Jackie Martin, Hannah Mortimer, Jill Murphy, Hannah Murphy, Philip Peatfield, Marion Porter, Anita Robinson, Anne Robinson, Judy Roux, David Rubra, Calie Shearer, Bernadette Simpson, Caroline Smith, Frank Smith, Sheila Smith, Geraldine Trussman, Helen Warburton, Michele Ward, Carole Warden, Dawn Weaver, Mary Welsh, Sheila Wolfendale and Caroline Woollett. Thanks also to Emily Perl Kingsley for permission to reproduce 'Welcome to Holland' (p8).

Thanks are especially due to Nic Watts who provided the illustrations.

My family yet again came up trumps with the necessary support and encouragement, and my partner David helped to keep the word processor and me on reasonably good terms throughout.

For Bettina Rallison

CHAPTER 1

Introduction

This book is about one of the most crucial factors in special education –
effective and empathetic communication.

Good communication, especially in the early years, is of vital
importance, and can make a significant difference to children, their
families and those working with them. It is essential both to ensure clarity
of aims and continuity of progress for the child and to promote
confidence in parents and teachers in meeting children's needs. Good
communication is about sharing aims, participation in decision making,
planning, reviewing and making the best use of resources. It is also about
reassurance.

How communication takes places is as important as the content. It has
a significant impact on what is heard and ultimately what happens for
each individual child. We are therefore concerned here about both the
content and the process of communication, how information is shared
taking account of contexts and especially the facilitation of partnership
with parents.

'It takes a village'

The much-quoted African proverb 'It takes a village to raise a child' is
especially true when it comes to children with special educational needs
(SEN). In Britain today, especially in urban areas, this 'village' is not so
much a group of neighbours as a whole community of professionals,
advisers, teachers and other workers who may be required to support the
family's efforts and help the child to make optimum progress.

Sometimes a child's special needs are evident at or soon after birth. For
many other families, the realisation that their child has a difficulty in one
or more areas of development dawns slowly. Whichever is the case, the

child's needs will become the focus for a number of adults who have a range of views, concerns and priorities. These individuals will come from some or all of the following groups:

- the parents and immediate family
- extended family and close friends
- others who will be caring for the child at home, nursery or playgroup
- medical or paramedical professionals such as health visitors, doctors, speech therapists and physiotherapists
- educational professionals such as teachers, pre-school coordinators, educational psychologists (EPs) and education support services
- Social Services personnel, who may include specialist social workers, daycare officers, workers in respite or holiday schemes
- other support services such as home support services (e.g. portage workers), a Named Person in a parent partnership scheme
- voluntary agencies
- special needs administrative officers within local education authorities (LEAs).

The child is part of a number of different systems, in which she lives and learns (see Figure 1.1). She is part of a family network, part of an education system, and a direct user of the Health Services. She may also be a direct or indirect user of Social Services. These systems overlap and interact at given points and at certain times. Some individuals in these systems are close to the child and may be in contact on a daily basis. Others are more peripheral but nevertheless exert an influence on what happens for the child as they are linked in some way to the systems and the people who support the child's development.

The various people involved form part of a wider system and, whether they realise it or not, each affects the other. When something happens in one part of the system, there will be shifts elsewhere. A mother who feels supported may have more emotional energy to interact positively with her child who may in turn respond more readily, and may make more progress as a result. A family who have felt uncomfortable with one professional may be more wary of the next one they come into contact with and there will be barriers to communication which again may have consequences all down the line. An early years worker who has fully understood what a physiotherapist has advised, and has felt able to clarify any uncertainties in a meeting, will be more skilled in adapting the environment appropriately for the child. The expectations and influence of a member of the extended family may influence how a parent sees his child, and this in turn affects how he perceives the advice given to him.

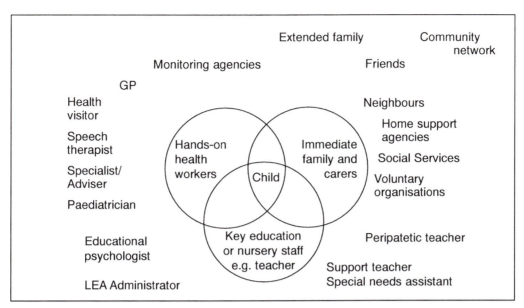

Figure 1.1 'The child is part of a number of different systems...'

Roles and responsibilities

Although all of these individuals would say that they want the best for the child in question, each has their own perspectives and priorities. They all have different roles and responsibilities and are operating within different contexts. Some are involved in order to make a particular kind of assessment and offer advice, others to work with the child to promote development; some will be more concerned with monitoring progress, others with supporting the family. Some, especially teachers, will see the child as one of many; whereas for the parent the child is the priority – but also part of the wider family. Some of these roles are multiple, others overlap and sometimes it may not be entirely clear who is supposed to be doing what.

It takes a determined effort to develop this potentially disparate and fragmented group of individuals into a cooperative team, who are able to communicate effectively with each other to meet the needs of the whole child within the context of his whole family and in a whole class group. The fact that traditionally professionals come from different disciplines, which have different organisational structures and different funding arrangements, has not helped. In many places, geographical boundaries are not in alignment and there is a need to work across local authorities. People may not know about the context in which other colleagues are working, and even the definitions used may be different. Some people, particularly in the Health Services, may see the child as having an innate problem that requires 'treatment', whereas many other professionals in Education and Social Services have a more interactive perspective.

'Working together' is seen as a much-valued concept in the literature and in the legislation but the reality is plagued with difficulties and there is a wide range of practice across the country. Many parents find themselves in the position of passing information around, sometimes at a time when they may themselves feel confused and unclear. Sometimes their confusion is exacerbated by the different information that they receive from different professionals.

Since the Children Act 1989 (DOH 1991) and the Code of Practice for SEN (DfEE 1994), there has been a greater effort to organise things differently to promote a higher level of collaboration. This has been emphasised even further with the introduction of Early Years Development and Childcare Partnerships. Much good practice, however, appears to depend on individuals who are deeply committed to the principle of inter-agency cooperation and many schemes are still in the early stages of development. Examples of good practice are given throughout the book. The legal framework is summarised in Chapter 2, and Chapter 3 gives a more detailed explanation of professional responsibilities within different disciplines.

Levels of knowledge and confidence

An important difference between these groups concerned with the child is the type and level of knowledge they possess about a child's particular needs, about the child within the family and about SEN procedures and resources. Knowledge gives rise both to confidence about what might be done to promote development and to appropriate expectations. Parents and carers may begin by knowing very little about their child's particular special needs but over time may become more knowledgeable than anyone else. In the early years, however, the plethora of assessment, advice and suggestion from many different concerned sources may only add to the feelings of anxiety, frustration, guilt and confusion that often beset a family who are learning to come to terms with and manage their child's special needs.

With the increased focus on providing a mainstream experience for children with SEN and including them in many of the activities and experiences that are open to others of the same age, more adults in early years settings are coming into contact with children who have a range of needs. In the same way that parents may be more or less knowledgeable and confident, this is also true for nursery officers and early years teachers. Where people are clearer about what is expected of them, and feel that they have the resources or support to do what might be required, it is easier for them to welcome children and their families warmly and positively.

With the family's agreement, it is also helpful if knowledge is shared about the whole child and the contexts in which she both lives and learns. A chance remark or suggestion, which shows little understanding about demands on the family or special needs procedures, can serve to increase guilt or raise unrealistic expectations that may generate frustration and conflict.

Development, progress and change

Any child's needs and development do not remain static and, especially in the early years, can change considerably over a few months. Good communication enhances continuity, especially during transition periods and when new people become involved. Chapter 6 is concerned with aspects of communication and liaison within a school or nursery. It also looks at what needs to happen when children move on. Good, regular, liaison ensures there will be a consistency of approach, evaluation of intervention, updated programmes, and that any new information is shared and taken into account when planning.

As some children with SEN may make very few steps over a review period of several weeks or even months, it is important that people hold on to the progress that children are in fact making. It is worthwhile to look back sometimes on progress made over longer periods so that everyone can be reminded of the results of their efforts. The annual review process for statemented children is supposed to do this but sometimes gets lost in the enthusiasm to plan forward rather than look back.

The importance of early intervention

All the recent legislation and guidance on children's SEN puts a firm emphasis on the importance of early intervention. There are some obvious reasons for this and others which are more subtle but equally important.

Promoting development

The more obvious reason for early intervention is that the earlier a child's needs are addressed and, where appropriate, programmes put into place, then the more progress the child is likely to make. Babies and small children, especially in the pre-school years, are at their most responsive and flexible, their brains more able to adapt to new ways of working. The younger a child is when intervention begins, the more chance there will be of making optimum progress – so long as the programme which is devised is appropriate for her developmental stage and suitable for her needs.

It is very important that the child is seen as a whole person and each area of their development is given attention. Where the child's difficulties and their remediation are the overwhelming focus for the entire family there is a danger that normal elements of functioning are ignored, possibly with negative consequences for the child's well-being in other areas. Collaboration and communication between parents, teachers and professionals will not only help to identify intervention, but also ensure that the child's needs are seen in the context of her overall development.

Maintaining the child's self-esteem

Self-esteem is not always the first thing that people think of when considering the importance of early intervention. When a child has inappropriate demands made on her however, and experiences failure on a regular basis she may develop a self-concept of herself as someone who 'can't' or 'is lazy' or who causes her parents distress. The child who experiences continual failure will eventually be reluctant to try and this will impede her progress even further. The earlier there is a good understanding of the child's difficulties and needs, the earlier there will be appropriate expectations and celebration of success when these are achieved. At the opposite end of the spectrum some parents are so protective of their child they do everything for her. These expectations are equally inappropriate and do not encourage the child to try things for herself and develop optimum independence.

Supporting parents

Emotional support

Much has been written about working in partnership with parents, but it is in these early days when a child's SEN are first identified that the interactions between the family and others are at their most crucial. The experience of having to face the reality that your child may in some way be different from others is potentially devastating. There is some evidence to indicate that not all parents have been told this news with the sensitivity that the situation requires (Herbert 1994).

Many families go through what can only be described as a period of grief. Like a bereavement, parents may go through stages of denial, shock, anger, guilt, overwhelming sadness and even depression before they are able to accept the reality of their child's special needs. For some families that point never really comes. The professionals who come into contact with parents, especially in the early days, may face some of these emotional responses and need to be prepared for them. Initial approaches to parents make a difference to how they view the professionals they will meet in the future. What is said to parents at this time also impinges on their feelings about themselves and their child. These include feelings of guilt that so often accompany having a child with difficulties, their anxieties about the future for their child and how she will manage and the future for themselves and how they will cope. There are also likely to be concerns about effects on the rest of the family.

Finding the right balance between acknowledgement of the parents' emotional response, the reality of the situation and being positive about the possibilities is not easy. The Royal National Institute for the Blind (RNIB) has published guidance for professionals about the way information is given (specifically for blind or partially sighted children) which includes the timing of this, the amount of information to give and the support parents need. Detailed and summary versions are available from the RNIB. Much of the advice is applicable to a range of SEN.

The strength of the support network for carers may be linked to the progress the child makes. Parents who can go to others who will listen, accept their child, not be judgemental, and offer advice and guidance when it is asked for may be better able to come to terms with what has happened and forge a more positive relationship with their child. Often this support network includes the professionals with whom the parent comes into contact, as well as the extended family, voluntary groups and other families. In some cases, it may be the entire support network the parent has.

It is important to remember that parents often have many other demands on them. The child who is the focus for the professionals is only one of a family's concerns and parents may worry about the effects on their other children. Working 'with' parents means being able to take into consideration not only what it is possible for them to do but also what is feasible. Unless parents are truly part of the decision making process they may agree to something that is in effect unrealistic. This may only serve to increase the guilt they may already be feeling and put further demands on an already overstretched family.

Figure 1.2 is a vivid analogy given by a parent to illustrate how it felt for her to have to come to terms with having a child with complex special needs.

Welcome to Holland
by Emily Perl Kingsley

I am often asked to describe the experience of raising a child with a disability – to try to help people who have not shared that unique experience to understand it, to imagine how it would feel. It's like this …

When you are going to have a baby, it's like planning a fabulous vacation trip – to Italy. You buy a bunch of guidebooks and make your wonderful plans. The Coliseum. The Michelangelo David. The gondolas in Venice. You may learn some handy phrases in Italian. It's all very exciting.

After months of eager anticipation, the day finally arrives. You pack your bags and off you go. Several hours later, the plane lands. The stewardess comes in and says, 'Welcome to Holland.'

'Holland?!?' you say. 'What do you mean Holland?? I signed up for Italy! I'm supposed to be in Italy. All my life I've dreamed of going to Italy.' But there's been a change in the flight plan. They've landed in Holland and there you must stay.

The important thing is that they haven't taken you to a horrible, disgusting, filthy place, full of pestilence, famine and disease. It's just a different place.

So you must go out and buy new guidebooks. And you must learn a whole new language. And you will meet a whole new group of people you would never have met.

It's just a different place. It's slower paced than Italy, less flashy than Italy. But after you've been there for a while and you catch your breath, you look around...and you begin to notice that Holland has windmills...and Holland has tulips. Holland even has Rembrandts.

But everyone you know is busy coming and going from Italy...and they're all bragging about what a great time they had there. And for the rest of your life, you will say, 'Yes, that's where I was supposed to go. That's what I had planned.'

And the pain of that will never, ever, ever, ever go away...because the loss of that dream is a very, very significant loss.

But...if you spend your life mourning the fact that you didn't get to Italy, you may never be free to enjoy the very special, the very lovely things...about Holland.

Figure 1.2 Welcome to Holland (©1987 Emily Perl Kingsley. All rights reserved. Reprinted with permission.)

Information support

As can be seen from the *Welcome to Holland*, it cannot only be distressing emotionally in these early days following identification, it can also be highly confusing. Professionals who spend their working lives in the SEN world do not fully realise that the structures, the language and the understanding which are so familiar to them on a daily basis are often completely foreign to others. The terminology itself is open to misinterpretation. Parents need to be able to ask the same things over and over again and it may be helpful if information comes from a variety of sources, including other families who have had similar experiences. Written guidance which parents can refer to in their own time can also be useful. Professionals need to take their lead from parents – too much information too soon may not be helpful as parents will be unable to take it in.

When a child's SEN are first identified parents may want the answers to questions that are difficult, if not impossible, to answer with any level of precision. They may want professionals to predict specific or long-term outcomes for their child or they may want to know exactly what support will be available. Sometimes professionals are reluctant to say that they do not know the answer to something for fear this may damage their credibility. It is, however, better to outline the range of possibilities, or the processes by which decisions will be made, than to give what appears to be concrete and substantive facts which are actually ill-informed, potentially misleading and raise inappropriate expectations. It may be tempting to tell parents what they would like to hear to alleviate their distress, but this only leads to greater grief later on and damages relationships with other professionals. It is also not helpful to outline all the potential difficulties at the outset as this may raise anxiety unnecessarily.

The last thing parents need at this time, however, is to feel that they are being kept in the dark in any way or denied information that may be useful. Even though they cannot be given definitive answers to everything parents need good, accessible information in a language they can understand. This could include some or all of the following depending on the special needs identified, the level and complexity of these, and who is most involved at this early stage:

- reassurance that the parents will be part of any decision making and intervention
- discussion of any immediate action that it is appropriate to take on behalf of the child and the rationale for this: e.g. observation over a given period, programme to develop certain skills, any referrals, etc.

- names and contact details of any relevant voluntary organisation
- contact details of any local support group
- if the child is in educational provision, a copy of the SEN policy
- names of individuals who will be the main contact(s) for the family and the arrangements for communicating with these people
- LEA SEN procedures where appropriate
- the range of provision that is available
- any criteria for accessing that provision
- review arrangements.

It is unrealistic to expect parents to take in a whole new range of information all at once. They do, however, need to know where to find out when they are ready to and to feel confident about coming and asking.

Family support

The family support service at Moorfields Eye Hospital in London was established over 21 years ago, and has a pivotal role for families in bridging the gap between a diagnosis of blindness or impaired sight in children and the real world of feelings and practicalities. The service is regarded by many in the community as an exemplification of good multi-agency practice.

Jackie Martin, the social worker who set up and runs the service, says that her central aim and philosophy is to empower families.

'Many are so strong – but they will flounder if they don't know where to go for help when they need it.'

In the early days, however, timing of information is important, as is the way it is presented. A lot of people telling families what their child won't be able to do and what they as parents should be doing isn't always helpful.

In the first instance, parents are often unable to take in all that has been said to them by doctors and need an opportunity to talk to someone away from the clinical setting. Jackie is able to explain what the diagnosis means and the implications for families. She is there to answer many of the questions that they may want to bring up and to help them focus both positively and realistically about their child's needs. She balances the medical model of diagnosis and treatment with the interactive model that looks at how the disabling effects of a visual difficulty can be minimised. Jackie's ability to support the emotional responses of parents at this time and to explain that their feelings are quite normal helps them come to terms with the situation and may well prevent later emotional difficulties arising. She also provides an informal counselling service for children who often have fears and anxieties about their treatment and condition. Jackie puts parents in touch with any support networks and, where appropriate, gives them information about their rights and how to access these.

In time, with written parental permission, Jackie liaises directly with other agencies, such as home visiting services and teachers for the visually impaired, who go into homes and schools to advise on specific approaches, materials and interventions. Having someone who has access to the detailed medical implications of the child's condition and who also has knowledge of the family is invaluable in planning and providing appropriate education and support. Information about how the child and family are managing can also be useful to those who are treating the condition in the hospital.

CHAPTER 2

The Legal Context

The people who work on behalf of children with SEN do so within a complex framework of legislation and guidance. Although everyone must take note of all the legislation, the emphasis for each person will depend on their particular profession and who employs them. In general teachers will work within the Code of Practice guidelines for SEN (DfEE; Circular 4/96 in Scotland, SOEID 1996), social workers and the health professionals within Children's Service Plans and pre-school providers with Early Years Development and Childcare Plans. There are increasing expectations that plans will be integrated with each other and be developed in partnership to provide seamless services to children and families. Figure 2.1 shows that legislation and guidance overlap in practice, and Figure 2.2 gives further detail of this.

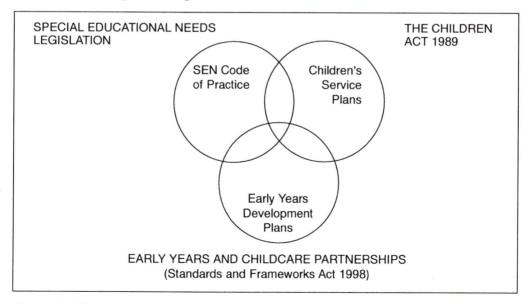

Figure 2.1 The interrelating legislation and guidance which inform practice

SEN LEGISLATION AND GUIDANCE

The Education Act 1981: Difficulties now seen as interactive and contextual, not residing wholly within the 'handicapped' child who needs 'treatment'.
It is the child's *needs* that are paramount.

The Education Act 1993 (Part 3) repealed the 1981 Education Act but retained its philosophy, clarified processes and strengthened its core principles. A special educational need is defined as a learning difficulty which calls for SEN provision to be made.

The Code of Practice (1994) provides guidelines for the operation of the Act (see Figures 2.3a, 2.3b and 2.4).

The Disability Discrimination Act 1990 requires all schools to report on admission procedures for disabled pupils. They have to make clear arrangements for physical and curriculum access and have proposals to prevent discrimination.

Excellence for All Children 1997 (Green Paper) and SEN Action Plan 1998 place a strong emphasis on early intervention, inclusive education, school responsibilities, partnership with parents and multi-agency collaboration.

THE CHILDREN ACT 1989

Among other things the Act requires the local authority to:
- identify children in need
- maintain a register of disabled children
- provide services which enable children in need to be cared for and brought up by their families
- provide services to enable children who are disabled to live as normal a life as possible
- publish information about the services that they provide for children in need
- listen to the views of children and their parents.

A child is deemed to be in need if his health (mental and/or physical) or development is likely to be adversely affected without the provision of services; either direct services for the child or services provided to the family.
Emphasis on services for children in need who are under eight, including day care, after school and holiday care. Local authorities are encouraged to support existing schemes, including home visiting services, voluntary organisations and self-help groups.

EARLY YEARS LEGISLATION

The Nursery Education and Grant Maintained Schools Act 1996 requires all early years providers, including private nurseries and playgroups, to have 'due regard' to the Code of Practice for SEN in the same way as schools do.

School Standards and Frameworks Act 1998 Early Years Development Plans. An early years place, albeit part-time, must now be provided for all four year old children whose parents want one – to be extended to four year olds. Plans must state the provision available to meet the SEN of pre-school children, with the expectation that an inclusive arrangement will be provided wherever possible.

All registered providers must offer a range of activities which encourage children to work towards the QCA Desirable Learning Outcomes. A qualified teacher should be involved in all settings providing early years education within the Plan.

Early Excellence Centres illustrate good practice in providing a high quality, integrated multi-agency early years service.

Figure 2.2 Brief summary of legislation and guidance

Themes of the legislation and guidance

Early identification

> Early diagnosis and appropriate intervention improve the prospects for children with special educational needs, and reduce the need for expensive intervention later on. For some children, giving more effective attention to early signs of difficulties can prevent the development of SEN. (DfEE 1997a)

The increasing acknowledgement that early support for children and families is likely to make the most difference to their future has led to an unprecedented focus on early years education and childcare. In addition to the early years initiatives outlined below, the Sure Start programme has been set up to provide support and guidance to more vulnerable families with babies and very young children.

Early years development and childcare partnerships

Plans drawn up by Early Years Forums representing all early years providers (not childminders) must demonstrate how partnership between the public, private and voluntary sectors will secure a government funded part-time pre-school place for every four year old whose parents want one. The integration of early years education with day care and out of school provision is a central feature of the plans which are designed to meet the needs of both children and their parents. LEAs have responsibility for ensuring that children are matched to places that best suit their needs. It is intended to extend this statutory provision, in due course, to all three year olds.

All registered early years providers are expected to work towards the desirable learning outcomes as specified by the Qualifications and Curriculum Authority (QCA). These are curriculum targets in personal and social development, language and literacy, mathematics, knowledge and understanding of the world, physical development and creative development. This early years curriculum, together with the baseline assessment which in England and Wales takes place within seven weeks of children starting reception class, is likely to contribute to the early identification of difficulties.

Registered early years provision is now the responsibility of the LEA rather than Social Services. All services for children which provide daycare under the Children Act 1989, however, are required to be regularly inspected by Social Services departments as well as by Education (DOH 1991). The Nursery Inspectors appointed by the Office for Standards in Education (OFSTED) are, among other things, responsible for looking at the clarity of roles and responsibilities within the early years provision and liaison with agencies. They are also interested in plans for improving the procedures for meeting the needs of individual children and improving partnership with parents and carers.

Early years providers and SEN

All early years providers have to provide information on:

- SEN policies and the facilities available
- staff knowledge and skills in dealing with children who have SEN
- links with organisations concerned with SEN.

They should appoint a member of staff who is familiar with the Code of Practice and able to support other staff on SEN and link with parents and outside agencies.

All early years providers are also subject to the Disability Discrimination Act 1990.

The Early Years Training and Development Fund provides funds for initiatives aimed at improving the knowledge and qualifications of all early years staff in nursery settings. This includes training for staff working with children with SEN.

Interactive and continuous assessment

Assessment no longer has an exclusive focus on the child's innate problems, but takes account of the child's strengths and personality and factors within the child's environment. Good practice, therefore, involves assessing the interactions between the child and others, what he is being expected to do, the difficulties he is experiencing, his response to intervention, the strengths he contributes and the contexts in which he is living and learning. Consequently, the emphasis in intervention is not so much on what the child should do as to what should happen in order for him to make progress. Ideally, an agreed programme should identify appropriate expectations, adaptations, activities, responsibilities, approaches, inter-agency and home–school communication, monitoring and review.

The Code of Practice on the Identification and assessment of Special Educational Needs (DfEE 1994)

The Code of Practice has become the special educator's well-thumbed handbook. LEAs and schools must have 'due regard' to the Code in the planning and delivery of services for SEN. This now applies to all registered early years providers. There is acknowledgement within the legislation that assessment is an ongoing interactive process and that an assessment, planning, action and review cycle is an appropriate format for the changing needs of children. The model of assessment as outlined in the Code of Practice is designed to ensure that assessment takes account of a child's response to intervention.

Section 5 of the Code of Practice: assessments and Statements for under fives

This sets out the procedures that must be followed. These differ somewhat depending on whether the child is over or under two years. See Figure 2.3.

A child who is identified as having SEN under the age of two is likely to have major health difficulties or a particular condition.

If a parent requests an assessment, the LEA **must** carry this out.

If the child's needs have been identified by others, such as the Child Health Services or Social Services, the LEA **may** carry out an assessment if the parent consents to this.

LEAs may carry out the assessment in the way that they consider appropriate. **Statutory procedures do not have to be followed.** Parents must be enabled to participate fully and children should be assessed in a place where the child and family feel comfortable.

Statements for children under two are rare and programmes of individual support should be considered in the first instance, such as home-based intervention. Careful monitoring of these will contribute to assessments after the age of two.

If a child is in a nursery class or school the procedures for identifying and meeting special educational needs are broadly the same as for school age children (see Figure 2.4).

Where a child is in a non-educational setting and there is cause for concern, clear documentation should be kept of the child's difficulties and any action taken to deal with those difficulties. This should include advice from any outside agencies.

If a District Health Authority or National Health Service Trust come to the opinion that a child under five may have SEN they must inform the LEA. Health Authorities must also give parents information about local statutory and voluntary services that might be able to help them. Such a notification from Health to Education ensures that the LEA monitors the progress of the child. It may, but does not necessarily, lead to a statutory assessment.

Where a statutory assessment is requested the LEA will assess the evidence that the child's difficulties or developmental delays are such that they require a multi-professional approach which includes monitoring and review over a period of time.

If it is decided that this is the case then statutory procedures are initiated. These are the same for all children. The contributions of non-educational service providers and parents are of key importance.

Figure 2.3 Identification and assessment of children over two but under five years

When a child moves into an educational setting a somewhat different set of regulations comes into operation with a staged process (see Figure 2.4). It is expected that this process should take place whether or not the child has reached statutory school age.

The school-based stages should be seen as a continuous and systematic cycle of planning, action and review to enable the child with special educational needs to learn and make progress.

Stage 1

The main responsibility lies with the class or nursery teacher.
An initial concern is expressed about the child and his ability to access learning.
The class teacher finds out more about the child by talking or playing with him, consulting parents, looking at school records and carrying out some initial assessment. She also discusses the child with the Special Educational Needs Coordinator (SENCO).

The child's name is put on the Register of SEN.
The class teacher makes some adaptations in the delivery of the curriculum and monitors the child's progress. A review with parents and others is held after about six weeks.

Several children in a class may be identified at Stage 1 as in need of something a bit different or more focused.

NB: There has been a recommendation in the SEN Action Plan that this stage be deleted.

Stage 2. (school support); The responsibility is shared between the class teacher and the SENCO, who now takes the lead in assessment, planning, monitoring and review.

If, after two reviews, the child is either not making sufficient progress or, following initial discussions with the SENCO, intensive early intervention is indicated, the child is placed at Stage 2.

The initial information gathered at Stage 1 is reviewed and further information gathered from Health, Social Services or other agencies involved with the child and his family.

Following discussion, an Individual Education Plan (IEP) is drawn up. This outlines the child's difficulties and the action to be taken to help him make progress. It should identify several short-term targets and who will be doing what, how and when. The plan should be implemented as far as possible within the classroom setting, using resources normally available. Parents should always be informed of actions the school is planning on behalf of their child.

A few children in a class group may require an IEP at Stage 2.

Figure 2.4 School-based stages

Stage 3. (school support plus); The SENCO takes the lead role and calls upon specialist advice external to the school.

If, after two reviews, the child is making minimal progress and more specific and detailed assessment and advice is required, the child is placed at Stage 3.

After consultation with parents specialist advice and/or support is requested. This could be from the Educational Psychology Service, an advisory teacher or the Support Services.

A few children in a school year may require outside agency advice and/or support.

Stage 4. (statutory multi-disciplinary assessment)

If, following two reviews at Stage 3, the child is not improving and seems to have long-term and/or complex SEN, a request is made by the school to the LEA to initiate a full statutory assessment. This request needs to be accompanied by relevant supporting evidence. Parents must be in agreement. Many LEAs now have criteria about the level at which statutory procedures will be initiated. If the process is agreed it should take no more than six months to complete. Advice will be sought from the child's parents, teachers, educational psychologist (EP), medical officer (MO) and anyone else who has been involved.

Only about 2 children in a 100 will have SEN at a level which may require a Statement.

The responsibility for meeting the child's needs is now shared between the school and the LEA.

Stage 5: (provision of a Statement of SEN)

Following the statutory assessment, the LEA decides whether or not to issue a Statement. If it does so, the Statement will summarise the child's strengths and weaknesses, identify needs and the provision that will be put in place to meet them.

This Statement must be reviewed annually to see whether it remains appropriate, should be amended or discontinued.

NB: There has been criticism of the 'stages' terminology as there is an assumption that one stage will follow another. 'Levels of need and support' is more appropriate and this is the recommendation of the SEN Action Plan. It is expected that as children make progress they will no longer require support at the same level.

Figure 2.4 (cont) School-based stages

The Lincolnshire COPPS procedures

The (COPPS) Code of Practice Pre-School procedures are now followed for all children, whatever the level of their SEN and whether they are in an educational provision or not. It helps to clarify children's needs over time, coordinate intervention and ensure that appropriate provision is made.

STAGE 1 is characterised by those people who might ordinarily be involved with young children and their families:

- parents/carers, health visitors, day carers, general practitioners (GPs), playgroup and nursery workers.

Where there is cause for concern about a child further information will be gathered, specific observations made and interventions planned on the basis of these. Review of the plan and outcome may lead to:

- maintaining or amending the current plan for the child and his family
- moving to Stage 2.

STAGE 2: This is characterised by the added involvement of one or more specialist agencies who do not routinely work with all or most children:

- speech and language therapists, portage workers, physiotherapists, occupational therapists, sensory impaired services, consultant medics.

Those who were involved at Stage 1 continue to be part of the Stage 2 action plans and reviews: for some children the evidence indicates the need to seek Stage 3 involvement.

With parental agreement:

- health workers may refer the child to the Community Health doctor (MO)
- portage workers or nursery workers may refer to the educational psychologist (EP).

STAGE 3: The aim of Stage 3 is to establish an overall coordination of the interventions into a plan–do–review cycle.

The MO and the EP have regular Stage 3 liaison meetings to discuss referred children.

At these meetings they coordinate and exchange information about:

- the child's needs and learning to date
- current provision – is this effective or should alternatives/ additions be sought?
- future implications for education.

They then:

- draw up a coordinated plan which clarifies what each will do
- agree who will consult with parents about proposed actions
- fix a review date.

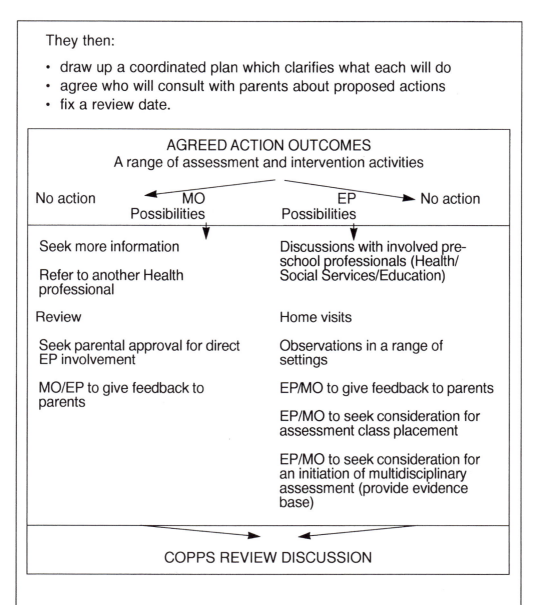

AGREED ACTION OUTCOMES
A range of assessment and intervention activities

No action ← MO Possibilities   EP Possibilities → No action

Seek more information	Discussions with involved pre-school professionals (Health/ Social Services/Education)
Refer to another Health professional	
Review	Home visits
Seek parental approval for direct EP involvement	Observations in a range of settings
MO/EP to give feedback to parents	EP/MO to give feedback to parents
	EP/MO to seek consideration for assessment class placement
	EP/MO to seek consideration for an initiation of multidisciplinary assessment (provide evidence base)

COPPS REVIEW DISCUSSION

These procedures promote good communication and coordination between the professionals involved with a pre-school child. They ensure that decisions are made on the basis of collated multi-agency evidence, that there is minimal duplication, that parents receive consistent information and that actions are regularly reviewed within the Code of Practice framework.

Information here relates primarily to England and Wales. There is related legislation in Scotland and Northern Ireland but details are different, e.g. a Statement of Special Educational Needs in English Law is called a Record in Scotland. The Scottish Office Education and Industry Department (SOEID) Circular 4/96 outlines the procedures for opening

---

Step 1 Identification of difficulties in learning

The teacher takes action to overcome the learning difficulties within a defined period, generally by adjusting the class programme. The teacher reassesses, making a record of the problems faced by individuals, and their learning strengths.

Step 2 Referral to learning support co-ordinator

Parents are informed and consulted. Additional assistance may be given to the individual by promoted staff, another teacher, or the learning support specialist attached to or on the staff of the school. Arrangements are made to review progress.

Step 3 Referral to support services outwith the school

Where it is decided that turther assistance is required, the head teacher may first seek advice from an adviser or learning support specialist from outwith the school. The next step is to seek parents' permission to refer the child to the psychological service.

Step 4 Consideration of the pupil's needs by the educational psychologist

A course of action is recommended in writing with, where approriate, advice on the content of the curriculum and learning and teaching strategies. Where action is some form of educational programme, arrangements are made for review and evaluation, in consultation with parents and school staff.

Step 5 Consideration is given to opening a Record of Needs

The head teacher, parents and, normally, the educational psychologist consider whether a Record of Needs should be opened. School staff prepare a report on their view of the child's strengths and needs.

Step 6 Medical examination and psychological assessment

The child is assessed. the medical officer and the psychologist prepare reports. Staff in school, meantime, continue to give the pupil assistance.

Step 7 Meeting to discuss opening of Record of Needs

The professionals, including representatives of school staff, meet with parents to discuss assessments. If the decision is that a Record of Needs should be opened, then the pupil's special educational needs are defined and the provision required to meet these needs is specified. School staff prepare or update their individualised educational programme for the pupil.

Step 8 Opening the Record of Needs

The Record is drafted and a copy is sent to parents for approval. Once approved it is 'opened' and copies are sent to parents, school and psycholocal service.

Figure 2.5 Steps to be taken in identifying and assessing pupils' SEN at the primary stage in Scotland

and managing a Record of Needs (SOEID 1996). Instead of five 'Stages of assessment' as in the Code of Practice there are eight steps as outlined in Figure 2.5. In the Children (Scotland) Act 1995 the definition of a child in need includes those who are affected by the disability of another family member as well as those who are disabled themselves (Gunner 1997).

Inclusion

The term 'integration' for SEN, which was commonly used throughout the 1980s and early 1990s, and is in fact the term used in the Code of Practice, is gradually being replaced by the term 'inclusion'. This gives the connotation of being part of something rather than additional to it, and takes account of all children rather than a few. One of the major outcomes of legislation over the last two decades has been the increased focus on the desirability of inclusive practices rather than the segregation of children with SEN. The White Paper *Excellence in Schools*, published in June 1997 states 'there are strong educational, social and moral grounds for educating pupils with special educational needs in mainstream schools' (DfEE 1997c). The Green Paper *Excellence for All Children* reiterates the Government's commitment to the principle of inclusion, though it does not say that this is appropriate or desirable for every child: '...we shall promote the inclusion of children with SEN within mainstream schooling wherever possible...' (DfEE 1997a).

The Children Act 1989, with its focus on family support to meet children's needs, aims to give children as near normal an experience as possible (DOH 1991). Both Children's Services Plans and the Early Years Development Plans must address how the needs of disabled children can be met by services in non-segregated settings wherever possible. The Schools Access Initiative is being expanded so that schools become more accessible to children with disabilities.

Many children with severe and/or complex needs are, however, still educated in special schools, albeit with increased opportunities for integration with mainstream peers. The Green Paper has proposed that structures are developed between special school and mainstream staff. This will not only support children re-integrating into mainstream school but also offer expertise to mainstream staff to enable them to meet varying educational needs.

The Nursery Education and Grant-Maintained Schools Act 1996 promotes inclusive practices for young children by:

- making it illegal for admissions policies to discriminate against children with SEN
- enabling LEAs to make resources available to private and voluntary early years providers to help them meet identified SEN.

Partnership with parents

Parental involvement, responsibility and inclusion in both decision making and service delivery is an integral part of all the legislation and guidance on SEN. Maintaining parental responsibility and rights is also stressed in the Children Act 1989.

The themes in *Excellence for All Children* (DfEE 1997a) and the SEN Action Plan (1998) are:

- empowerment; which encourages parents to work closely with schools and local services in order to identify and meet a child's needs as early as possible
- entitlement to information about what is being provided for their child in school
- partnership; including the expansion of parent partnerships and 'Named Person' schemes
- parental choice about their child's education – including the right to opt for a special school rather than a mainstream placement or vice versa
- access to LEA mediation for dealing with disputes.

Unfortunately, the rhetoric has not always been matched by practice because of inherent conflicts within the legislation. Parents naturally want what is 'best' for their child and LEAs have to provide what is 'suitable', taking account of factors that include the needs of other children and the most effective use of resources. Parent partnership schemes are, however, increasingly operational throughout the country and will soon be in place everywhere.

The 'Named Person' scheme, intended to support parents of a Statemented child, has often been helpful at the beginning of the Statementing process, enabling parents to participate more effectively. The involvement of parents at earlier stages of the Code of Practice has been less evident. There are proposals to improve the operation of school based SEN provision and disseminate good practice in working with parents. Parent partnership schemes in the future will provide advice and independent parental support from the earliest stages of identification. In Scotland a national SEN advice service is being set up with effect from April 1999.

The involvement of children

The Children Act 1989 emphasised the rights of the child to have their feelings and wishes known and taken into account when decisions are made about them (DOH 1991). The SEN Action Plan (1998) proposes to strengthen the guidance in the Code of Practice to encourage LEAs and schools to seek and take account of the child's views (DfEE 1994). The Children (Scotland) Act 1995 further expands the rights of children to attend hearings that are about them (Gunner 1997). Anither significant difference in this act is that the definition of a child in need includes those who are affected by the disability of another family member as well as those who are disabled themselves.

Multidisciplinary and inter-agency working

The need to communicate, collaborate and coordinate has been a strong theme throughout the legislation. There is increasing recognition that collaboration between organisations and agencies needs to be at the structural level as well as in response to individual needs and that links must be strengthened between Health, Education and Social Services. It is acknowledged that there has been a history of fragmentation and competition between departments which has led to parents having to coordinate services for their children. The Government accepts that responsibility for improving communication begins with the DfEE's SEN Division. There has been a promise to provide information, commission research and disseminate good practice.

The way forward

The needs of children have had an increasingly high profile over the last decade and there is continued pressure on services to raise quality and work more effectively. In response to these various pieces of legislation there has been a concerted effort to improve coordination of services for young children. In many local authorities, provision has expanded with consequent demands for training and monitoring of quality. Partnerships are developing, both with parents and between agencies. Although there is still a long way to go, the expectations about the way forward are now clearly laid down.

Woodlands Park Centre of Excellence

Woodlands Park is part of Haringey's Early Excellence Network, comprising three early years centres, two of which were among the Government's first cohort of seven centres of excellence. The centre offers a flexible use of 80 full time equivalent places, responsive to the needs of the community. Fifteen places are reserved for children with a developmental or family need and about 25 per cent altogether have an identified SEN. The SEN support assistants are permanent members of staff rather than attached to individual children. 'They are part of everything that is going on here, they know the rest of the staff and the parents really well so there is continuity and shared good practice.'

The principles of inclusion and partnership are firmly embedded within the policy and practice of the centre. Carole Warden, the head teacher, is in no doubt about the advantages of having a community focused provision.

> Parents respond very positively to the fact that this is not a stigmatised setting – it helps them come to terms with the long-term nature of their child's difficulties. We have a focus here not just on the child but on the whole family.

Outreach and drop-in services are central to the ethos of the centre. Julian Grenier, deputy head and SENCO, says that it is of great value to families when they can just come in and talk to the person they want to see. Sometimes a chat with a visiting professional is all that is needed and is an excellent use of time. Joint training, sometimes including sessions for workers and parents together, is also seen as a highly worthwhile enterprise and a sensible use of limited training budgets.

The positive, welcoming ethos of Woodlands Park is tangible both for children and their families. The excellence lies not only in the high level of skill and innovatory practice but in the warmth and understanding that underpins all activities and developments. The chart opposite summarises these.

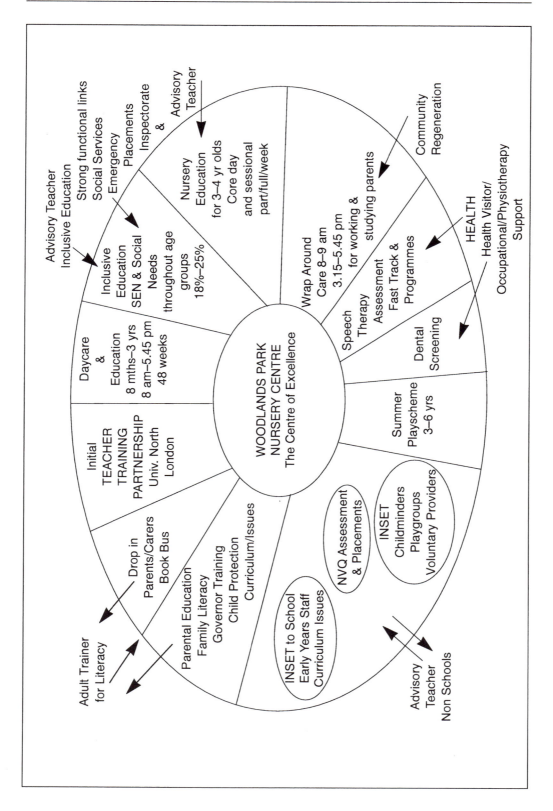

WOODLANDS PARK NURSERY CENTRE
The Centre of Excellence

Advisory Teacher
Inclusive Education

Strong functional links
Social Services
Emergency
Placements

Inspectorate
&
Advisory
Teacher

Nursery
Education
for 3–4 yr olds
Core day
and sessional
part/full/week

Inclusive
Education
SEN & Social
Needs
throughout age
groups
18%–25%

Daycare
&
Education
8 mths–3 yrs
8 am–5.45 pm
48 weeks

Initial
TEACHER
TRAINING
PARTNERSHIP
Univ. North
London

Drop in
Parents/Carers
Book Bus

Parental Education
Family Literacy
Governor Training
Child Protection
Curriculum/Issues

Adult Trainer
for Literacy

INSET to School
Early Years Staff
Curriculum Issues

NVQ Assessment
& Placements

INSET
Childminders
Playgroups
Voluntary Providers

Advisory
Teacher
Non Schools

Summer
Playscheme
3–6 yrs

Dental
Screening

Speech
Therapy
Assessment
Fast Track &
Programmes

Wrap Around
Care 8–9 am
3.15–5.45 pm
for working &
studying parents

Community
Regeneration

HEALTH
Health Visitor/
Occupational/Physiotherapy
Support

CHAPTER 3

Roles and Responsibilities: Who Does What?

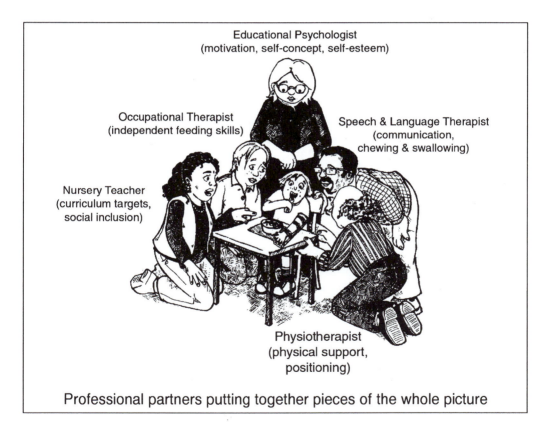

Educational Psychologist
(motivation, self-concept, self-esteem)

Occupational Therapist
(independent feeding skills)

Speech & Language Therapist
(communication,
chewing & swallowing)

Nursery Teacher
(curriculum targets,
social inclusion)

Physiotherapist
(physical support,
positioning)

Professional partners putting together pieces of the whole picture

One of the necessary features of good collaboration is clarity about what different professionals do, how they do it and with whom. This helps to ensure that there are appropriate expectations, little duplication and fewer inappropriate referrals. It also means that everyone knows where to go for specific advice and guidance.

Many services have leaflets for parents that give a basic overview of what can be expected. In best practice, these are translated into community languages. Some services provide open information for everyone about what they provide, how they work and how they can be contacted. Others offer information that is more limited. Inadequate information, however, can lead to assumptions and raise false hopes. Transparency about services, which defines terms and is unambiguous, is usually the best option.

Casework and consultancy

One misconception about how professionals work is the extent to which they will be involved in 'hands-on' casework. Although specific interventions are often necessary, what is equally important is the overall approach and interaction that children experience on a day-to-day basis. The professionals will assess a child's needs and identify appropriate strategies to promote development but they will not necessarily be the people providing all the delivery. Not only do services not have the resources to do this, but interventions are also less intrusive when they happen in a routine way with familiar adults. It is, therefore, likely that the professionals will be consulting with parents and teachers about ways of meeting the child's needs at home and school, as well as offering a direct service when this is indicated.

The discrepancy model

Some hard-pressed services operate what is termed a 'discrepancy' model. This is where a child will be given priority if they have a difficulty which is specific rather than part of an overall delay, i.e. there is a discrepancy between their skills in one area and their skills overall. The rationale for this model is to target resources for children who are likely to make the best use of them. There is usually, however, an emphasis on providing services for the early years where intervention is likely to have the most effect on longer-term outcomes.

Variations in service delivery

Although this chapter gives a general overview of roles and responsibilities, not all services operate in the same way. There are wide regional variations, both in the resources that are available and in the specific activities that are undertaken. We are also living in a time of considerable change and development, with new legislation – both recent and proposed – in special education, early years provision, and community health. It would be wise to check with local services for details of how they work in your area.

Coordination within services

As well as improvements in multi-professional collaboration for SEN children and their families, there is also a need for greater clarity and improved communication between different services in the same department. Managers need to consider how all the agencies for which they are individually responsible:

- centralise referrals
- plan together to make joint decisions
- offer discrete services which prevent duplication
- give consistent rather than conflicting messages
- communicate effectively with each other.

Coordination of services appears to be facilitated by sharing premises.

The real world

Although the aim is for clarity and consistency, good inter-agency work often depends more on positive working relationships than on rigid role definitions. Best practice is where professionals focus on the needs of the child and family, share what has to be done and decide jointly who is doing what. People who are hidebound by their job description may be lacking the flexibility that working with complex situations might need. Planning must be based on what is the sensible thing to do for this child in this situation with the resources and skills that are available.

When people share the responsibilities, the challenges and the solutions, they gain a better understanding of both the pressures others are working under and the possibilities that exist.

More information about the roles and responsibilities described below can be obtained from the professional organisations listed in Appendix 1.

Health professionals

The health visitor

Health visitors are primary health workers for the under fives. They are crucial both in the identification of children with developmental needs and in early support for families.

All health visitors are registered nurses and may have a degree in community health.

At present, health visitors are usually employed by community health trusts, but it is anticipated in the future that primary care groups will be the budget holders for their services. They may work closely with GPs and with clinical medical officers (CMOs) in health clinics. There is often a specialist health visitor for children with special needs attached to the child development centre (CDC). This person does not take over from the family health visitor but will support and work with her where necessary.

Health visitors are informed by special care units of any child who is born with a specific difficulty, such as Down's Syndrome or spina bifida. Communication comes either from the paediatric nurses or the liaison health visitor. Local health visitors are also informed about any child who has been admitted into the accident and emergency department. Health visitors are also responsible for visiting families who are new to the area, whatever the age of the children.

At the first home visit, the health visitor will ascertain the kind and level of support the family will initially require. This will depend on many family factors, not just the specific needs of the child. If the baby has a medical need, a paediatric nurse may remain the health keyworker for longer.

Health visitors are jointly responsible for a programme of developmental surveillance. Checks are carried out at the following ages:

- 6 weeks   – carried out by a doctor
- 9 months   – health visitor
- 18 months   – health visitor
- 3 years   – health visitor
- 4 and a half years   – doctor

Many difficulties in one or more areas of a child's development are identified at these checks. Records are kept in what is known nationally as the 'red book'. There is also a 'hand-held' record kept by the parent who is given responsibility for taking this to other medical professionals.

Individual health visitors make judgements about the need to refer on, which they cannot do without parental permission, unless this is to Social Services in relation to a child protection issue. If the child needs to be seen by a paediatrician or medical specialist, this must be via the GP or the CMO. Health visitors do, however, make independent referrals to paramedics such as speech and language therapists and other agencies, such as home visiting services.

Health visitors provide a range of support services for families where there are children with a disability or other special need. This may be on an individual basis with the health visitor making regular home visits, by giving information about voluntary groups or by referring to under fives provision or peripatetic services.

When a child with SEN enters school the health visitor will liaise with the school nurse and in some instances may attend an intake planning meeting.

The general practitioner (GP) – also referred to as the 'family doctor'

Every family should be registered with a local GP – often this will be with a group practice/health centre rather than with an individual doctor. GP practices are fundholders, and, therefore act as gatekeepers to specialist medical services. They often have contracts with local hospitals which may limit the choice of where referrals can be made.

Many GPs are now involved in their own developmental surveillance and clinics are held regularly at surgeries. Health visitors may be attached to several GP practices and be responsible for all the children who are registered with those particular doctors. Referral to the CDC will be via the GP after discussion with the health visitor. GPs may also refer in response to direct parental concern. Where health clinics are not attached to GP practices referrals will be made by the CMO attending the clinic.

Once referrals have been made and the child's specific needs are being monitored elsewhere, GPs are usually no longer directly involved except with general healthcare and any crisis intervention. Any health specialist who becomes involved with a child should ensure that reports are sent back to the GP.

Some family doctors are well tuned in to current philosophy and practice for children with special needs but others have little awareness of the educational context. As GPs often have very close links with families and may be seeing them on a regular basis, it is important to promote inter-agency understanding in order to prevent parents inadvertently being given misleading information.

The community paediatrician/child development centre or unit

Most Health Authorities have a CDC or unit, which is responsible for the assessment of children whose development is giving cause for concern. Some of these assessments will be multidisciplinary. Although the majority of referrals are for children under five, they do see children of any age.

The community paediatrician is the doctor in charge of the CDC. He or she coordinates a team of medical professionals, such as doctors, speech therapists, occupational therapists (OTs), physiotherapists, clinical psychologists, and specialist health visitors. Decision making meetings may be coordinated in the CDC involving other professionals such as educational psychologists (EP) and social workers.

The community paediatrician is usually the designated medical officer (MO) for SEN. This includes responsibility for:

- ensuring that a child is referred to the LEA if it is considered that he or she has, or is likely to have, special needs which will require special educational provision to be made: the decision making process and criteria for this referral differs within different areas as does the liaison between the CDC, other health professionals and other agencies
- coordinating statutory medical advice, within the expected time limits, for assessment which may lead to a statement of SEN.

The community paediatrician will also refer on to appropriate specialists as required.

The School Health Service

School Health Services take over from health visitors as the health-monitoring agency for children once they are of school age.

The school nurse

The school nurse works with CMOs as part of the school health service. All schools have an allocated school nurse, although the visiting schedule may differ considerably from one institution to another. Often it is the health visitor who will liaise with pre-school provision about individuals, but the school nurse may also be able to offer ongoing support, especially if the child is in a nursery attached to a school.

School nurses are well placed to give specific guidance for all children with particular medical needs, from asthma to enuresis, and to advise staff who will be in contact with these children on a daily basis. Where there are initial concerns about vision or hearing school nurses can carry out basic checks. They may also have initial discussions with parents who have not sought other appropriate medical advice. Along with health visitors they are valuable professionals to include in an intake or transition meeting for a child with SEN who also has medical needs which require awareness, monitoring and/or intervention.

School nurses have knowledge about non-accidental injury and are able to advise teachers on what to look out for and when to be concerned.

As well as monitoring and advising on specific issues, school nurses have always had a role in health promotion. Their brief extends to the mental well-being of children and young people as well as their physical care.

The audiologist

The audiologist is a doctor who has specialised in hearing development and difficulties. Nearly all hospitals where there is a CDC will have an audiology clinic. Children will be referred there if they are communicating well below the level expected for their age. Although this is not always due to hearing difficulties these may either be a contributory cause or need to be eliminated.

The audiologist tests children on 'pure-tone' measures that indicate whether there is impairment in one ear (unilateral loss) or two (bilateral loss). Often, even where there is a difficulty in both ears, there will be different functioning in each. The audiologist will be able to say whether the child has difficulty hearing high frequency sounds (mostly consonants such as 's', 'f') or low frequency sounds (mostly vowels and the less sharp consonants such 'm', 'n'). He or she will also be able to tell how loud the sound has to be before the child can detect it. This information is summed up in a chart called an audiogram. The peripatetic teacher for the hearing impaired will be able to interpret an audiogram and let parents or teachers know what the difficulties mean for the child and her learning. Audiologists routinely refer children to this service.

The audiologist will also be able to tell whether the child has:

- a sensory-neural loss which is an impairment of the internal mechanisms for hearing and may be permanent
- a conductive loss due to temporary blockages
- a mixture of both.

He or she may refer the child for specialist treatment and/or may prescribe hearing aids.

The orthoptist and opthalmologist

Orthoptists and opthalmologists are doctors who have specialised in different aspects of vision. The orthoptist is primarily concerned with functional eyesight, how well the child sees through both eyes (binocular vision) and the muscle balance involved. He or she is concerned with the large variations within otherwise normal eyesight. The monitoring of a child with poor vision would be part of their role, together with remediation such as glasses and exercises to develop better vision. The opthalmologist is more concerned with pathology – the health and disease of the eyes. If the child has a condition that requires treatment or surgery then an opthalmologist would be involved. Sometimes both specialists would need to work together for a child with complex visual difficulties. Othoptists may refer to educational and other agencies who would be involved in maximising functional vision, but it is very unlikely that opthalmologists would do so.

Child and adolescent mental health

There are behavioural issues for many children with SEN, and a number of different agencies may become involved. When parents are in agreement for a referral to be made to a mental health team or specialist service, they are likely to have already had contact with other sources of support and advice.

A child and adolescent mental health team will comprise all or some of the following:

- a child psychiatrist, who is a qualified medical doctor specialising in paediatric mental health; this person will have responsibility for any medical diagnosis. If any drug therapy is recommended it has to be via a qualified medical practitioner. If it appears there is an underlying medical condition, he or she may refer to a paediatric neurologist or other specialist.
- a clinical psychologist; this person is not a medical practitioner although may have the title 'doctor' following his or her own professional qualification. The psychologist will be involved in assessment, in counselling families and in consultations about the management of the behaviour. He or she may liaise with teachers, and other professionals.
- a psychotherapist; this person is not a doctor. He or she may have trained in working with individuals, groups and/or family therapy. Psychotherapists usually work within a particular model (way of thinking about why difficulties arise) which informs their practice.
- a community psychiatric nurse who will make home visits where appropriate.
- sometimes there is an attached social worker who has a mental health responsibility.

The child and adolescent mental health team may provide all or some of the following:

- clinical assessment, which attempts to ascertain the underlying reasons for the child's difficulties
- individual therapy sessions – with or without parents
- family therapy – where the emphasis is on understanding family dynamics and the meaning the child's behaviour has in this context
- play-based therapy – to allow individual expression, problem solving and aid further understanding
- family support – aimed at management of the behaviour at home and helping families with their feelings about having a child with difficulties
- drug intervention where considered appropriate
- referral to further specialist services.

The speech and language therapist

Speech and language therapists (SLTs) are trained to work with children and adults to assess, diagnose and treat those with communication and some eating problems. They are either graduates in speech sciences or have completed a two-year post-graduate qualification. Many SLTs, especially those trained more recently and those working with children, will have a good knowledge of the educational context, special needs and relevant legislation.

SLTs work with children who have:

- difficulty in producing and using speech sounds
- difficulty in understanding their own language
- difficulty using language
- a stammer or other voice problem
- swallowing or eating difficulties as a result of trauma or developmental delay.

Although most SLTs are employed by Health, an increasing number of those in child services are funded by Education, especially where they are working in special schools or classes or with statemented pupils in mainstream. They work with parents, teachers and carers, providing advice and support as well as assessment, diagnosis and treatment programmes. SLTs will tend to take an interactive view of difficulties with the aim of promoting optimum communication for the individual child. They have a strong liaison role with other professionals and will often offer training for those working directly with children.

Speech and language services tend to prioritise the early years for intervention and pre-school groups for children with speech and language difficulties are offered by many Health Services. The criteria for admission often depend on the specific difficulties the child is experiencing.

Speech and language services usually have a referral system that is open to parents and professionals alike. Children who are referred to their local CDC for developmental difficulties are likely to see a SLT as part of this overall assessment.

The physiotherapist

Physiotherapists usually complete a three to four year degree course and then specialise. Physiotherapists have expertise in physical development and work under a doctor's authorisation. Although most referrals are from GPs, paediatricians and other consultants, some services for children have an open referral system under the guidance of the community paediatrician. A physiotherapist can become involved with a child and her family right from birth. At this stage, giving support to parents is considered as important as giving advice on how to handle the child.

As well as working in clinics, CDCs and special schools, many paediatric physiotherapists work within the home, especially where children are under three. Health visitors may identify the need for a physiotherapist to be involved because of difficulties the child was born with and/or because parents require guidance and support in promoting their children's physical development. Social deprivation may limit children's access to necessary experiences, such as crawling around. Some conditions require physiotherapy treatment to prevent or limit physical difficulties arising.

Physiotherapists need to work closely with many other professionals. Physical development and movement is dependent on vision, hearing and communication skills. Physiotherapists refer to and liaise with home intervention schemes to develop joint early years programmes.

When children enter nursery or school, physiotherapists can advise teachers and special needs assistants about access to play and especially the positioning a child requires to access activities. Where muscle tone is weak children need physical support, and where muscles become rigid children need help to achieve flexibility. It is important that there is consistency of approach between home and school. Physiotherapists can advise schools of equipment they need to purchase, and are sometimes able to provide things on loan. Special schools for physically disabled pupils will have an allocated physiotherapist.

Although there are considerable overlaps between the role of the physiotherapist and occupational therapist, concerns about mobility and larger motor movements would initially be referred to the physiotherapist and concerns about fine motor skills, eye-hand coordination and perceptual skills to the occupational therapist.

The occupational therapist

Occupational therapists (OTs) are graduates and are state registered. Their training gives equal stress to the two components of psychological and physical needs. The central belief of OT philosophy is that activity is central to a person's well-being. An OT is therefore interested in:

- activity as a therapeutic tool
- ensuring that optimum activity is possible for individuals.

The skills and role of an OT are very far-reaching and can range from such activities as assessment of what is needed to help a child who has difficulty in feeding herself independently to play therapy for traumatised children. OTs are employed by Health Services, Social Services and by some voluntary agencies.

OTs employed by Social Services assess what is needed to enable someone to carry out the normal functions of everyday living. The outcome of this assessment will be advice, training and equipment, including at times adaptations to the home. In general, if the need for equipment is medical, e.g. necessary for a child's well-being or development, then it is the Health Service who are responsible for provision. If the need is functional, i.e. without specific equipment the child cannot carry out the necessary activities of everyday living, then it is Social Services that are responsible for provision. Equipment solely for use in school is funded by Education and not assessed by a Social Services OT.

Referrals can be made to the social services OT team directly by parents or professionals. Social Services OTs liaise with Health paediatric OT services but would rarely visit schools.

OTs who are employed by the Health Service work in hospital departments, special schools, the community and specialist centres. Access to OT services for children who are in mainstream schools is variable.

In some areas, referrals to paediatric OTs must come through a doctor, others have an open system. Although paediatric OTs work with children and young people of all ages, most give priority to children under five years. They are concerned about how a child's presenting problem impacts on function. They are involved with children who have acquired difficulties following accidents or other injury; who have conditions such as cerebral palsy or muscular dystrophy; or who have problems arising from orthopaedic problems, developmental delay, dyspraxia, and specific perceptual difficulties. They may also be involved with a wide range of other difficulties, including children of small stature or other vulnerability whose ability to function normally is affected without adaptations to the environment. Where advice is given to schools, it relates to how a child's motor or perceptual difficulties will affect their learning and the strategies that can be employed to minimise this. This includes how work is presented. OTs may also offer some general advice about specific needs, e.g. developing pencil control.

Paediatric OTs work in partnership with parents and multidisciplinary teams, especially physiotherapists. They often liaise with home visiting services.

Education professionals

Apart from teachers and nursery officers, there is a range of different education professionals who are involved with schools. They include link inspectors, school and pre-school support services, EPs, school effectiveness teams and advisors. They have diverse roles in quality monitoring, whole-school development, staff support and meeting the needs of individual children. None of these roles is exclusive and each affects the other. Collaboration between these services to offer seamless support to schools and consequently children is closer to reality in some LEAs than in others.

Portage and other home visiting services

Although portage has been listed under Education, the funding and management of such services varies widely. Some are funded and coordinated directly by Education, others are Social Services based and some organised by Health. Many are jointly funded. Portage workers often work closely with other agencies.

Portage (named after the town from which it originated) is a well established method of intervention for young children with SEN and their families. Portage workers will all have gained the initial Portage Certificate and many will have received advanced training.

The aim of portage is to empower parents to be the most effective teachers of their children. Families are referred through a number of agencies, most commonly through health visitors. Portage workers visit families on a regular, usually weekly basis, offering a highly structured intervention programme. Following assessment, parents agree a learning target with the portage worker. They work together on this and then the portage worker leaves behind an activity chart to record daily intervention and provides related toys and other equipment on loan. Families usually continue with the service until the child has made sufficient progress or is spending a substantial amount of the week in an early years provision.

Other professionals will often make joint visits with portage workers and this may contribute to the action plans for the child.

As well as the basic and advanced training, the National Portage Association provides a range of training courses related to children with special needs, such as quality play courses. This training may be offered to those working in pre-school settings as well as home visitors.

Other home visiting services offer a much less structured input than portage and may see their role as offering more general support and counselling to the family.

The educational psychologist

There is a Psychology Service in every LEA. Educational psychologists (EPs) are psychology graduates with a further higher degree in educational psychology. Most will have had teaching experience. The role of the EP is presently being re-evaluated by the DfEE and guidelines will be published following consultation.

EPs are involved with children from 0–19 years and a significant part of their work is with the early years. They work in partnership with parents, teachers and other professionals. EPs usually make regular visits to provision rather than on a referral basis and are able to provide consultation on general issues as well as for specific children. This could include devising strategies for managing behaviour, training for working with parents or advice on policy development for SEN. Although EPs may get to know individual families well over time, they rarely work directly with individual children on a long-term basis.

Health Authorities have a statutory obligation to inform Education about a pre-school child who has or may have SEN. The LEA will often ask the Educational Psychology (EP) Service to respond. Sometimes the family will already be known to an EP, but if not further information will be gathered and usually an initial home visit will be made. The EP will usually carry out some informal assessment by observing the child and talking with parents. He or she will discuss the family's concerns and wishes, clarify the involvement they have already had with other services and provide general information about educational provision. EPs give their views about children's needs to the LEA, who make any decision about further assessment and/or provision.

When a child's SEN are first identified after she has started school or nursery, an EP will become involved at Stage 3 of the Code of Practice (school support plus) (DfEE 1994). The EP will usually work with others to refine specific programmes of intervention. Should the LEA be asked to initiate a statutory assessment there should usually be evidence that the advice of the EP has been sought and acted upon.

The EP can be a useful resource for both parents and early years workers. He or she will have a wide range of knowledge about aspects of child development, learning and SEN. EPs are familiar with SEN procedures and can provide information about these, the variety of provision and services that may be available and about the processes involved in access. They may also be able to judge the extent to which the child meets any criteria that have been set up for different levels of support and be able to indicate what are realistic expectations.

EPs often have some first-hand knowledge of the many contexts in which the child is living and learning. This potentially gives them a strong liaison and coordination role between parents, educational providers and other services.

EP Services frequently provide training. Ask your EP Service about what is on offer.

School support teams

School support may include:

- advice and training for particular SEN
- advice about the needs of individual children
- specialist in-school teacher support
- special needs assistants (known by different names in different LEAs).

School support teams have various forms of organisation. In some LEAs the funds are delegated or devolved to schools who employ additional staff or purchase support hours from a central service. At the present time some services remain centrally funded and both teachers and support assistants are provided at Stage 3 (school support plus) to Stage 5

(Statemented pupils). Some services are very large, with different teams who are allocated to specific needs, e.g. language team, behaviour team, or to different phases of education. These teams often establish close working relationships with other professionals. The training and supervision that can underpin the work of a centrally based team raises the quality of the support available. The advantage of school based support is that it can more easily be arranged to fit in with the curriculum and other aspects of school life.

An evaluation of school support is central to annual and other reviews.

Outreach workers

Strengthening the links between mainstream and special education has been recommended in *Excellence for All Children* (DfEE 1997a). There is a view that skills that are presently based in special schools should be disseminated more widely and used to promote inclusion. There are various models of outreach work, which may be combined:

- support for individual children and their mainstream teachers especially at transitions
- advice and training
- a resource base within the special school which is open to mainstream teachers
- two-way group or class integration with children transferring between special school and mainstream.

The peripatetic service for the visually impaired

All LEAs should have access to a service for the visually impaired. Many boroughs share a service – a good example of regional collaboration. Sometimes a person with expertise in working with children with visual impairment will be part of a more generic support team. It is often the case that a child with impaired vision will have other developmental difficulties.

Peripatetic services are part of education and staffed by qualified and experienced teachers, most of whom have a qualification as a teacher of the visually impaired.

Services usually operate an open referral system but will require parental agreement and medical information before they become involved. Parents are asked to give written permission to the service so that the orthoptist or opthamologist can be contacted. In some cases where there are delays in getting this the visual impairment (VI) teacher may make an initial home visit to explain their role.

During an initial visit for a pre-school child, the VI teacher will be doing the following:

- finding out the parents' main concerns
- assessing the child's functional vision – the use the child is making of the sight they do have and the adaptations they are employing
- assessing awareness of light and dark, making eye contact, hand-eye coordination
- explaining and interpreting medical information to the parents in terms of implications for the child and the family
- assessing other aspects of the child's development and needs
- deciding on priorities to help the child develop their residual vision most effectively.

When a child enters an educational provision it is important that the staff make contact as soon as possible with the VI Service, as they are an invaluable source of information and support. The VI teacher will be able to explain the child's difficulties in terms of what it means for their learning and the implications this has for adapting the environment and developing specific approaches. This includes materials, print size, positioning, mobility, access to activities and so on. Some services are able to loan equipment to schools or, in the case of Statemented children, recommend items that the school needs to request from the LEA.

The extent to which a peripatetic teacher will be directly involved with a child will depend on each child's needs and the extent of their disability. Teachers or nursery officers closely involved with the child require access to VI teachers and the SENCO needs to disseminate relevant advice throughout the school, including those who supervise at lunchtime.

The peripatetic service for the hearing impaired

All LEAs should have a peripatetic service for hearing-impaired children and their families, though this may vary in size and may be part of a sensory impairment team. The staff in these services are all qualified teachers who have also completed an additional training which gives them a recognised qualification as a teacher of the deaf.

In most cases, referral to the service is via Health, especially the local audiology clinic, but referrals are taken from any agency.

Where young children are involved, the teacher would visit the family in the first instance. They would discuss the implications of the findings of the audiologist, discuss the use of hearing aids if these have been advised and talk about other services that may be available. Where appropriate they would work with other home visitors, such as portage workers. Follow-up visits would be arranged as required, sometimes with other family members so that information is shared with all those who have contact with the child. Over 90 per cent of children who are significantly deaf are born to parents with no hearing impairment. It is often useful, therefore, for parents to meet with a deaf adult who can provide them with some reassurance about their child's future development and opportunities. The peripatetic service may arrange this.

When a child goes into early years provision the peripatetic teacher will be able to discuss exactly how a child's hearing is impaired and the implications this may have for their play, education and social interactions generally. It is important to discuss functional hearing. The sense that the child may make of language in a lively classroom may be different from that in a room with optimum acoustics.

If a child has significant difficulties, the peripatetic teacher will liaise regularly with the following:

- the audiology clinic
- the SENCO within the school or nursery
- the Speech and Language Therapy Service – perhaps a specialist within that service
- the educational psychology service
- others who may be directly involved with the child either because of hearing or other needs
- the person who will be responsible for monitoring the day-to-day use of hearing aids (and their batteries); this could be a member of the support staff.

The peripatetic service focuses on raising teacher awareness of the needs of children who do not hear well, both for individuals and for general practice. For young children in particular, good practice for children with hearing difficulties is good educational practice for all children – such as ensuring children are looking at you before speaking to them and giving visual support for new vocabulary.

The peripatetic service will usually provide a monitoring role for children with a hearing impairment throughout their school life; how often they visit will depend on the child's specific needs and the level of support they are receiving from other agencies.

The LEA Named Officer (administrator)

When it is proposed that a statutory assessment of a child's SEN should be initiated the LEA informs the parents. The information given includes the name of the person in the education office who will be responsible for overseeing the process. If the parent, or anyone else, has any queries, it is this person who should be contacted. The Named Officer is primarily an administrator and usually does not have the authority to make decisions on behalf of the child. He or she can, however, pass concerns and requests on to decision making panels.

If there is a difference of opinion between the family and the LEA, it is sometimes the Named Officer who meets with parents to seek agreements. There are some LEAs where Named Officers and parents meet to discuss the content of the Statement once it is drawn up, or even beforehand to clarify what the parents might expect to be included.

Once a child has a Statement, there is a continuing need to ensure that monitoring and review take place. The Named Officer will maintain the file and keep copies of annual reviews. On occasion, actions by the LEA are required, such as when it is recommended that a child's needs be met elsewhere. The Named Officer will usually oversee the administration of that process.

The Named Person (sometimes known as a 'befriender' or parent supporter)

This is someone that the LEA must identify when sending parents out the final version of a statement. The Named Person must be someone who can give parents information and advice about their child's SEN. The Code of Practice suggests that he or she be identified in cooperation with the parents. Named Persons may be appointed at the start of the assessment process and support the parents through this, encouraging their participation.

Unlike the Named Officer, the Named Person is not someone directly employed by the LEA. All LEAs should have now set up a Parent Partnership Scheme, which is responsible for the development of the Named Person scheme. In some LEAs a voluntary organisation has taken on this role. Many of the Named Persons are volunteers although the organisation of the scheme, including recruitment, training and support, is funded by the LEA. There has been a recommendation to extend this scheme for all parents of children with SEN to give them access to an independent parental supporter.

Social Services

Many social workers will be social science graduates and most have a Diploma in Social Work. Until recently Social Services Departments

(SSDs) were usually organised into area teams, but they are now increasingly likely to operate in specialist teams, e.g. services for children and families, for the elderly, for people with mental health difficulties. While SSDs deal with the whole age range, they have distinct statutory responsibilities for identified children. These are children in need, children in need of protection, children 'looked after' and children with disabilities. SSDs have a major responsibility in relation to assessment. They are purchasers of services as well as providers, and provision may be commissioned by SSDs to meet assessed needs.

The educational social worker (educational welfare officer)

In some authorities this service is managed by Social Services and in others it comes under Education. The role of the educational social worker (ESW) is traditionally in connection with school attendance. Where their role is broader they may be asked by schools to make a home visit where there is any concern about the welfare of a child. They can often offer useful advice where there is an initial concern about child protection. ESWs have a potentially strong role in liaising between home and school where children are looked after by the local authority.

Children with disability

SSDs have a major responsibility for the operation of Children's Services Plans for children under eight and children with disabilities. A child who has an identified disability or other special need should be offered an initial visit by a social worker, for an assessment of their needs within the family.
   This might be for:

- practical support, such as respite care
- financial support; some children may be entitled to a disability living allowance (DLA)
- adaptations to the home (see the section on OTs)
- daycare provision – either within an early years provision, e.g. Under Fives Centre or separate, e.g. a supported childminder place
- advice, training and information.

Parents are encouraged to put their children's names on the Children with Disabilities Register. This gives them access to regular information about such things as holiday schemes and support group activities and it also helps services to plan for future needs.

Some SSDs have specialist social workers for children with disabilities. These may be within area teams but are often attached to CDCs or special schools. In these settings they work closely with other professionals.

Child protection

Many schools and nurseries come into contact with Social Services in connection with child abuse concerns. All education provision should have a designated link teacher and each local authority has statutory guidelines for monitoring and referral procedures. Some services provide a drop-in facility for all professionals involved with children to discuss their concerns in the first instance. Where child protection is an issue, social workers should be invited to all inter-agency education review meetings and teachers to all Social Services case conferences and reviews.

Child and family (consultation) services

Known by different names and sometimes run in conjunction with Health services and/or the voluntary sector, this service offers family support using counselling and therapeutic approaches. It is often used by families who are worried about emotional difficulties their child may be experiencing and/or where there may be problems in managing their child's behaviour. Referral procedures may vary, but where Social Services are the sole organisers, a family may have to be referred by a social worker. Sometimes family support services are offered more informally in early years settings.

Family group conferences are a recent innovation and present a different model of collaboration between families and professionals. They are intended to help families problem solve their own difficulties. Used mostly for families where there is a child in need, they are often set up in conjunction with Health and Education. The aim is to support families in devising family based solutions to problems rather than rely on professionally-led decisions.

Voluntary agencies

Some of the numerous voluntary agencies related to SEN are listed in Appendix 1. Voluntary agencies can be either local or national, and either umbrella organisations such as those campaigning for inclusive education or for specific difficulties. They have a significant and increasing role in the education and support of children with SEN and their families at several different levels. Voluntary agencies may provide, coordinate or contribute to the following:

- information, e.g. publications, conferences, training programmes
- family support, which is usually provided by local groups; these may be generic, e.g. a 'children with disabilities' group or branches of national organisations for specific difficulties, e.g. AFASIC (Association for all Speech Impaired Children)
- respite support, such as Familylink – usually provided in conjunction with Social Services
- individual advice and support; national organisations can give advice for specific issues, parent partnership schemes are usually run by voluntary agencies and can provide individual supporters
- educational provision; the voluntary sectors provide schools or classes, mainstream and special. Several organisations, such as Homestart, provide early years home programmes for general difficulties and others for specific difficulties, e.g. motor impairments or autistic spectrum disorders. Often parents have to contribute towards the cost of this input or seek funding elsewhere.
- LEA policy making; representatives of the voluntary sector are increasingly consulted or even invited to participate in policy making
- pressure groups; these use the media, conferences and other events to raise the profile of the changes that they would like to see
- research and training; major national organisations are often involved in carrying out research activities within the remit of their concerns. Sometimes they decide on areas of investigation and bid for funding, at other times government departments or universities may ask for their contributions.

It is important for all professionals to be aware of local group support for children and their families and to ensure that parents are informed about them. Where voluntary agencies are involved in direct work with children, it is helpful for professionals to liaise. A discussion about the advantages and drawbacks of different approaches will ensure that the parents have full information on which to base their future decisions.

The Voluntary Agencies Directory – from the National Council for Voluntary Organisations (NCVO) lists all registered agencies: Tel: 020 7713 6161.

Summary

This chapter illustrates the wide range of different people that may be involved with a child and her family. Some of these roles are distinct but many overlap. This needs to be seen as a strength rather than a potential source of confusion – but it will only be if people communicate and work closely with each other. This is particularly crucial when any planning takes place. Joint decisions between parents and professionals about who is doing what to support the child, the family and the school must be a first step.

Poppies: Professionals Operating with Parents to Provide Intervention and Early Years Support

Set up by the pre-school service in Newham and run by an early years teacher, a portage worker and a nursery nurse specialising in sensory impairment, Poppies is a weekly group for parents and their children. These children, who have a variety of complex SEN, are welcome from birth until they are regularly attending an early years provision.

Parents are offered a range of multi-sensory play opportunities to help their children develop skills in listening, communication, vision, large and small body movements and social awareness. Professionals introduce the activities as families move round different areas and then encourage parents to take over the interaction, commenting on and interpreting the learning experience. Recording is done together as an integral part of the activity. There is an open invitation for therapists and other professionals to come and join in. Many do so, seeing it as an opportunity to work in a different context with families. Sometimes they offer training or consultation to the whole group.

Margaret, mother of Lauren, a child with Down's Syndrome, is enthusiastic:

> We hardly ever miss a week, it's so nice to come together and you can see little differences in the children. People can be so competitive about their children and here whenever someone does something new it's lovely to celebrate it together.

Abida is a young mother who had just started coming to Poppies. Her son Hamza is eighteen months old and has a serious brain deformity. His

---

many difficulties include severely impaired vision and a specialist teacher attends the session too. This is how Abiza felt about it.

This is really helpful – some of the things I have learnt here I do at home and that really helps Hamza. He likes playing with the other children and now he can focus a little bit he loves the lights and the bright baubles that are hanging up. I see lots of people at hospital and the child development centre but before I felt all isolated being at home. I get support coming down here and seeing the other parents.

After the individual session, there are group activities such as songs and games. Many of these are interactive, to encourage the children's awareness of each other. Everyone has a drink and a chat before going home at lunchtime.

Cyril, father of Brendan, a child with cerebral palsy and West's syndrome, shares information about some SEN computer programmes, and everyone talks about the fun they have had with their children in the soft play room that they visit together once a month.

Newham has a pre-school team comprising teachers, nursery nurses and a senior portage worker. Poppies is one of three groups that are run by the service, which also offers a home visiting service, training programmes, and support for inclusion into mainstream early years settings. Close links are maintained with the CDC and contact made with all relevant professionals on receipt of a referral. Seven languages are spoken by members of the pre-school team, including British Sign Language.

CHAPTER 4

Early Identification and Communication with Parents and Carers

This chapter has three parts. The first two discuss different ways in which children's early difficulties may be identified in nursery or school and the implications this has for approaches to parents. Part 3 looks at some specific issues involved in establishing good home–school communication.

Part 1: Special Educational Needs identified by nursery or school

When a reception class teacher or nursery officer begins to have some concerns about a child and how they are getting on in school, they may wonder if they are right to be worried. Alternatively, they may feel surprised or even angry, that 'no one has picked this up before', especially when the difficulties are more apparent.

Clarifying concerns

The first thing is not to jump to conclusions about a child or act too hastily. Although early intervention is desirable there is no point in intervening, perhaps inappropriately, before there is some clarity about what is needed. Observing the child in different situations over a few weeks and presenting different activities to see how he approaches them will give a lot of information. Watching interactions with other children, seeing how he communicates; the level and complexity of play and doing things with him will give a much better idea of what the child can actually achieve with and without help. It will also identify more precisely the nature of his needs. If a notebook is kept somewhere accessible it is easy to jot down observations and comments without this being an arduous additional responsibility. Over time these brief entries will provide a wealth of information on which to base discussions about the child's needs with parents, colleagues and other professionals.

Avoid a 'deficit model'

It is possible to imagine a notebook containing numerous entries saying things like 'Patrick sat doing nothing all morning' or 'Ayse can't put her coat on by herself'. This may all be true, but does not say anything that helps to inform future action. If an entry read 'Patrick was seated at the sand tray and watched other children play with the sand', you know something about the context he was in and about his learning. If it also said 'When I sat with him to build a sandcastle he watched me. He was unresponsive to sentences but responsive to single words and gestures. He laughed as we knocked the sandcastle down together', you know how he responded to adult intervention and have some idea about the level of his receptive language. Similarly, 'Ayse can bring her coat to an adult and can put her arms in the sleeves if the coat is held', lets you know that she is aware of what to do, can follow a routine and has the physical ability to manage that activity. It is much more useful to think about a child as able to concentrate on a favourite activity for two minutes than to say that he cannot settle to anything at all. It facilitates more constructive communication with parents and others, and also provides a starting point from which to aim for realistic targets.

The learning and behaviour overlap

Although concerns are often raised as a result of 'hard to manage' behaviour this is frequently an integral part of other difficulties. Thinking about behaviour within a special needs framework helps those working with the child to maintain an appropriate professional perspective rather than taking the difficulties personally and feeling de-skilled. Clarifying behaviours for cooperation, independence, attention and play will help to discover whether:

- the child is showing immaturity in most aspects of his development and his behaviour overall is more like that of a younger child
- the child needs more physical outlets for his level of energy
- frustration with communication difficulties is a major cause of his behaviour
- the child appears emotionally distressed – reacts strongly to perceived slights and/or is often angry or tearful
- the child needs positive reinforcement to learn behaviour which is required in school or nursery: he will then especially need to learn that he will get attention by behaving well
- there is a more specific difficulty indicated by 'clusters' of behaviours.

It is easy to quickly attribute behaviour difficulties to poor parenting skills but, as can be seen from the above, there are many reasons that a child might present challenges in a busy classroom. Where parents do have more limited skills or are not coping well they need support, not condemnation. Expectations for the child may need to be changed.

Taking time to accept that a child has a special need

If the child's development is noticeably delayed in one or more areas, the chances are that the doctor or health visitor has indeed recognised that there is a problem and may have tried to address this with the child's parents. They may have actively resisted the notion that their child was not progressing along the usual developmental path, and refused further investigation or intervention.

Some families will not have had much contact with health professionals and little experience of other children. Finding that there is a concern about their child may come as a shock.

Other families recognise that all is not well but prefer a 'wait and see' approach.

When appointments are made without full parental support the family may simply not attend. Their reluctance may stem from having experienced a lack of sensitivity and from feeling blamed or guilty as well as having a struggle to accept their child's difficulties.

Unless there are serious child protection concerns professionals must wait until parents themselves request help for their child. It is useful to maintain a dialogue with the family, however, and hope to facilitate acceptance of the child's needs over time. This will be more likely to be fruitful if everyone is non-judgemental and supports the child and family to the best of their ability in the meantime.

Reasons for denial

When parents have little experience of young children, they may find it hard to both realise and accept that their child is different in some way from others of the same age. In some families, there sadly continues to be a stigma in having a child with difficulties and a lot of effort may be put into not acknowledging the existence of problems, especially within the wider family network. This may also be the parents' way of handling their feelings of grief, guilt and even shame.

In some ways, it may be easier for families to accept difficulties when these are more obvious and visible. Children who have communication and/or social difficulties may have experienced excellent development in most areas until they are about two years old when the difficulties begin to become more apparent. This not only makes it harder for parents to accept there is something wrong, but also makes others less understanding and even condemnatory, particularly about any associated behaviour difficulties.

Parents may acknowledge that their child has difficulties but be reluctant to discuss them for fear that their child will be 'labelled'. They may worry that negative things will be written about him, that these will go on his file, that this will affect how he is seen by others now and in the future and that this may limit his opportunities. It may help to establish partnership with parents if they are initially offered informal meetings to discuss their child's needs, which are not recorded. When these are positive and action-focused, parents may be reassured.

Messages parents receive about their child's special needs

The language that is used by professionals is vital in helping parents come to terms with their child's needs. Words like 'handicapped' and 'backward' are alarming and no longer exist within the special educator's vocabulary. This is because difficulties are seen as interactive and are described in terms of the child's needs. Not everyone is aware, however, of current philosophy and terminology, nor are they always knowledgeable about the possibilities of inclusion. Doctors may, with the best of intentions, give the impression that a child will not 'cope' in a mainstream school when, in fact, this may be entirely possible. Parents may then not always be fully open about their child's needs when they go to register him for a school place for fear of rejection.

The early experiences that parents have in discussing their child's needs can make a difference in how they perceive their child, their child's education and the possibilities for future collaboration with other professionals.

One of the phrases that is in common parlance, by special educators as well as the medical professionals, is 'developmental delay'. This means that a child has a difficulty, which may be long-term. The word 'delay' however, can be very misleading for those who are not familiar with this specific usage. Delay suggests 'catching up' and sometimes this is what parents and even teachers will be seeking – the time when the child is at the same level as everyone else. Children who are developmentally delayed certainly make progress but at their own pace. Looking for an intervention or a level of support which will reduce the gap between their skills and those of other children may be inappropriate and lead to disappointment. The focus must be on seeking optimum progress for each child, and celebrating their incremental successes.

The child entering school or nursery

When the child enters school or nursery, far from 'nothing having been done' there may, in fact, be a lot of history concerning the child's developmental needs. This makes it even more important how the child's needs are raised with parents. Giving them lots of facts about how the child is not managing will only serve to reinforce their fears and anxieties, and this may make if hard for them to 'hear' what is being said about their child's needs and what might be done to meet them.

Approaching parents in the first instance

There are no hard and fast rules as every family is different, but the following format should help teachers or nursery officers to think through their communication with parents/carers, whether there is a significant difficulty or a more minor concern.

Ask to have an informal discussion – perhaps a word at the end of a session. 'Have you got a minute – there's something I would like to ask you?' is better than immediately saying you are worried.

Start the conversation by saying something positive about the child. This is important for several reasons:

- it shows the parent that you are relating to the whole child, not just in terms of his difficulties
- it relieves their anxieties that the child will immediately be 'labelled' or even worse 'excluded'
- it shows some commitment to the child and that you are not only concerned about management
- once the parent's attention is secured there is more likelihood that the rest of the conversation will be heard.

Ask the parents if they have any concerns about their child's learning.

If they say that they do not then you could be more specific, e.g. 'I've noticed that J. seems to need/be struggling with/isn't always able to … What happens at home?'

You could then say something like 'I'd expect most children of this age to be doing... it looks like he needs a bit more help to get there'.

If the parents continue to resist acknowledging the difficulty you could ask them if it was all right if you just kept an eye on the child and we could see how he got on for a few weeks. Few parents could object to this – it is not so different from what would be happening anyway. You then have the opportunity to set up a review meeting.

If the parents are able to say that they also have concerns you may be able to talk more fully about what these are – take your lead from the parent, this may be a very difficult interaction for them. You could ask them if anyone else has mentioned problems to them. If it is appropriate, you may feel able to ask the parent if you could have their permission to contact their health visitor or other involved professional for information. It will be necessary to get this permission in writing, especially for any medical information. Some parents may, in fact, be quite relieved that their own nagging worries about their child's progress are being clarified. They may welcome the opportunity to share their concerns and pleased to know that something is being done.

It is a good idea to end the meeting with a plan of action, even if it is simply gathering more information, finding out more about how the child is doing in specific situations or putting in a minor intervention such as having the child sit close to an adult at carpet time.

A review meeting a few weeks on will ascertain whether there is a concern that requires more substantive assessment or support. At this meeting you could ask how the parents feel their child is getting along, what they think his strengths are as well as the difficulties he seems to be experiencing.

Moving on

If the teacher considers that the child's needs do require further intervention then the Code of Practice Stage 2 (school support) (DfEE 1994) comes into operation. The teacher discusses the child with the SENCO who should also try to meet with the parent to let them know what will be done to help their child.

Although partnership with parents is a cornerstone of special needs legislation, and should be promoted wherever possible, it is not necessary to get parents' permission to put in-school support programmes into place at Stage 2. Parents should, however, always be informed of what is happening for their child in school. Permission is needed for Stage 3 (school support plus) and no agency will become involved with a child without parental permission. They can, however, give general advice to the school on management for the particular difficulty a child is presenting.

Regular formal reviews of the support that has been put in place will help to clarify strategies that promote progress for the child. These should be regularly shared with the parents so that they continue to hear positive things about their child. Paradoxically this may help them, in time, to accept the difficulties and work in partnership with the school and others. At this point parents may agree to referrals that will access the services of other appropriate professionals.

It is very helpful if school staff have written information about services which they can give to parents, which reassures them about what to expect. EPs and other professionals who are visiting early years provision regularly would usually be pleased to meet with parents to explain their role and answer any queries. Parents may be reassured by this meeting and feel more comfortable about the professional's involvement with their child.

Part 2: Special Educational Needs identified by parents

The previous section looked at concerns that were predominantly teacher led, and the interaction between parents and teachers focused on developing positive communication so that full collaboration could eventually take place.

This section is about concerns that are predominantly parent led, where parents are anxious that their child is not making sufficient progress at school and want teachers to take their concerns seriously. In their interactions with schools, parents naturally want their views to be respected. Even if the teacher does not share the same initial concerns, they need to think about developing a framework in which useful home–school communication can take place.

It is often the case that a parent is the first one to notice that their child is struggling. They may be alerted to this by:

- comparisons with other children
- the child not being able to settle and concentrate on learning tasks
- the child not being able to do the work that is sent home
- the child being unhappy in school
- the child's behaviour becoming difficult to manage.

The early years curriculum

Parents may have expectations of what their child should be doing and learning which may not always be appropriate. This may be because they have an idea of what 'school is for' even if their child is only three. The recent debate about early years education may be contributing to parents' anxieties about the development of their child's skills. Where schools and nurseries take the trouble to show parents the educational value of the activities that are on offer this can be reassuring. Parents may not realise the many ways small children learn and the vital importance of play and self-directed activity as well as guidance to develop basic skills. Close communication with parents, not only about what takes place in the classroom but the rationale behind the activities, will also empower parents to support their child's learning at home.

Expressing a concern

Parents expressing a concern may do this in several ways. Sometimes it may be hard to get at the root of what they are trying to say. This could be for many reasons:

- they do not have the same terminology or even the same language as the teacher
- they are anxious, do not want to appear pushy and are hesitant
- they are unsure whether they should be worried or not
- they tend to adopt a certain manner when dealing with anyone they perceive is in authority – this may range from demanding their rights to being very 'respectful'
- the worry they have is complex and they don't know where to begin
- although anxieties are being expressed about their child in school, there are other worries about what is happening at home
- they have experienced a difficult time at school themselves or they have had negative experiences with older children and perhaps feel they have to make a fuss to be heard.

Sometimes parents may start off with a mild expression of concern and become increasingly outspoken if they do not see anything happening as a result.

Teachers might feel that there is an attack on their competency. Although it is hard to see through a negative approach, it is useful, at least in the first instance, to try to focus on the anxieties being expressed about the child. If parents feel that someone is really listening to them they may be reassured that their concerns are not being ignored and a more useful dialogue may ensue.

Listening

Parents have a right to express concerns and it may be useful to give written as well as verbal information about when teachers are available for a private discussion. It is more likely that parents will mention their concerns in passing and teachers can then offer to meet with them to talk it through properly.

The process of this discussion is important. It needs to be as free from interruptions as possible. A notice on the door and the 'phone off the hook helps. Checking out how long people can stay ensures that time is left to plan what to do.

Parents need to be put at their ease and encouraged to talk. Questions that are fairly open-ended will usually elicit information, but if the parents are having difficulty expressing themselves then more closed questions may help them out:

- 'What has been bothering you?'
- 'How long have you been worried about him?'

It is not a good idea to interrupt parents at this stage to tell them that everything is all right in school; it may be perceived as dismissive. It is better to prompt in order to find out as much as possible about why the parent is worried. The focus of the concern may change as the story unfolds.

Even if the teacher truly believes that the child is progressing well, parents may not feel that their concerns have been acknowledged unless there is some action from the meeting. Alternatively, parents may very well have identified a difficulty of which the teacher had been unaware. This meeting could conclude with one or more of several options:

- keep an eye on him for a few weeks and have another meeting
- find out more about the concerns expressed
- contact other professionals who may have been involved
- devise a home–school programme to address some of the concerns.

Under the Code of Practice (DfEE 1994), the child would be placed on the SEN Register at Stage 1. It will be helpful to make sure that the parents have a copy of the school's SEN policy so that it becomes a point of joint reference for future decisions.

Whatever the agreements a review date should be set.

'How well does your partnership policy work in practice?'

Finding out

If the child is in a pre-school provision, initial information can be gained from looking at his progress against the desirable outcomes measures. Likewise, if he is in infant school, the baseline measures will be useful.

In infant school, parents may be particularly worried about their child getting to grips with literacy. It would be wise to check out some pre-reading skills to identify any underlying problems with eyesight or hearing, especially finer skills such as visual and auditory discrimination. Can the child identify rhyme? Can he see small differences between pictures and symbols? Checking early language development and any family history will also give an indication as to the likelihood of literacy difficulties arising.

Teachers may like further guidance about what might be involved in difficulties with early reading processes, what to look for and how to go about it. A first step after consultation with the SENCO might be to ask an advisory teacher or the EP. Most services would be pleased to do this and would not require the referral of an individual child.

Emotional development and learning

It may be that the child is not progressing as well as he might because of an emotional difficulty. Worries about things at home, bullying by other children, anxiety about getting things wrong may all be contributory factors. Asking parents if any of these factors could be present is the first step.

Parents are often unaware of the links between emotional development and learning. Family breakdown or bereavement is often not discussed with small children who suddenly find themselves without a significant person in their lives. They may be very confused, think it must be their fault, need a great deal of reassurance, have poor concentration or become angry and badly behaved. It is common for children's attainments in school to suffer as a consequence – giving already distressed parents something else to worry about.

These issues may be very difficult for parents to talk about in school unless they have a particularly close relationship with the teacher. Having some general guidance available may therefore be helpful. Again, the EP Service is a useful contact for advice on these issues.

Moving on

It may be that the picture changes as a result of early investigations. Further tests of hearing or sight or other referrals may be indicated.

It may be appropriate to move to the Code of Practice Stage 2 (school support).

Parents who have raised the concern themselves are usually willing to be part of a home–school programme. It is likely that such programmes are already in place to some extent for all the children in the class. A more specific one for the child in question might be appropriate under the following conditions:

- it provides opportunities for the child to receive positive attention at home
- it aims at reinforcing learning rather than introducing new concepts

- it is enjoyable and not stressful for both parent and child
- it is not onerous for the parent who has problems fitting it into a busy schedule
- it helps parents to understand their child's learning better.

Negotiating what is possible for the parents, what is needed for the child to maintain motivation, and how the programme will be reviewed are all necessary components of a successful home–school intervention.

Seeking resources

It may be that the parents want individual support for their child and will come into school with the view that they need to 'fight for their child'. Following the listening suggestions as described above is the first step. Explaining carefully the school's policy and ways in which assessments are carried out and linked to a plan – do – review cycle of intervention may also help. It is not useful to talk to parents about the needs of other children or the stresses on teachers – it is their child who matters to them.

Good communication means close involvement with parents who can see what is being done, and are part of the solution. Once it is clear that their concerns are being taken seriously, initial assessments and investigations carried out and plans put into place, most will be reassured.

A very few parents, however, will see their child as the next Nobel prize winner and being held back by teachers who are not addressing his specific difficulties. They may want resources that are not available for their child's level of need and be less than responsive to a considered approach. There is no easy answer to this except to:

- acknowledge their natural concerns in wanting the best for their child
- be very clear how the school SEN policy links to the DfEE guidance
- share the information on which decisions are made
- provide information about what is done in the class to promote skills
- give information about support groups
- talk about activities or make reference to books or programmes which may support and extend their child's learning at home
- keep open the lines of communication wherever possible
- provide regular information about the child's achievements and progress in all aspects of the curriculum
- link attainments with the well-being and development of the whole child
- think about the time issues involved and make appointments to see the parents which have a structure, a beginning and an end.

Part 3: Specific issues in communicating with parents and carers

Language and cultural issues

Communication and collaboration with many families is affected by cultural and language issues. This is not simply addressed by having access to interpreting and translation services although that is better than nothing. Families from different ethnic backgrounds, especially if they are new to this country, may have very little understanding of the educational context, let alone all the processes and terminology surrounding special needs. Some LEAs and schools have made videos showing what goes on in school and have provided commentaries in community languages.

In some cultures, having a disabled child has different or additional meanings to those that might be expected. The level of shame, for instance, might be shocking to those with a western ideology and it could be easy to be judgmental about this. Working with local communities and encouraging a two-way exchange of information is useful. Where possible, translations of materials and information should be done in conjunction with people from local communities. It is easy to make cultural errors even if the translated language is correct.

For strict Muslim families, it is not acceptable for women to be in the presence of a man other than their husband unless the husband is also present. This may present difficulties in setting up effective home–school communication and may mean that some families require a more flexible approach.

The following examples of good practice show ways in which better communication might be established with families of children with SEN.

The Newham Bilingual Co-worker Scheme

Most professionals rely on translation and interpreting services to help them in situations where there is a language barrier to communication. These services, however, are not always available. In reality, it is often family members or friends with a little more understanding of English who provide interpretation. Both official interpreters and others may not have the contextual understanding that aids meaningful communication and may sometimes inadvertently give misleading messages both to professionals and parents.

The Newham Bilingual Co-worker Scheme was set up to address some of these difficulties in working with communities who had very little understanding of English. The professionals also felt they needed better cultural knowledge of families. The scheme has now been running for about eight years, predominantly in the Speech and Language Therapy Service but also now in other departments.

The scheme employs bilingual co-workers who are fluent in the main community languages in the borough and also have good skills in English. They are also required to have a thorough knowledge of the particular cultural group with whom they will be working. Advertisements to recruit staff are placed in the local press and via community organisations.

Although the role of the bilingual co-worker includes interpretation and translation it is much wider than this. In the Speech and Language Therapy Service, the co-workers are trained to carry out basic language assessment in the mother tongue. They then contribute to the diagnosis of the difficulties and in the management plan. They will be involved in mother tongue remediation and also in the preparation of appropriate materials. An important part of their role is to act as a cultural resource for the speech and language therapists (SLTs).

The main aim of the service is to empower families. It helps them to understand more fully what is being offered and supports them in making their needs known. Although used primarily in the early years the scheme also extends to school aged children.

Haringey's Community Development Project

This project, initially funded by Section 11 funding, is based within HINTS (Haringey Home Intervention Scheme) in the Children with Disabilities and Special Needs section of Haringey's Social Services Department.

There are three part-time community development workers who work within the West African, Turkish, Kurdish and Asian communities and sessional workers from the Somali, Polish, Albanian and French speaking African communities. Their role is to link with community associations, Health, Education and Social Services agencies to:

- ensure that families with children with disabilities are identified and referred to appropriate services
- ensure that relevant information is made available and accessible to families
- encourage families to place their children on the Children with Disabilities Register
- enable the home intervention scheme and the named worker project to offer a service which is responsive to the linguistic and cultural backgrounds of the families in these communities
- empower parents to be part of the consultative process in planning for children
- set up support groups.

Anyone can refer to the project, and leaflets that explain what it is about are available in community languages.

The community development workers are not employed as interpreters, but will make joint visits with other agencies when their knowledge of a family and their culture makes this appropriate. The aim is to link families into appropriate support systems and then withdraw.

Communication with both parents

Under the Children Act 1989, both parents have rights and responsibilities, even if they are not living together (DOH 1991). At present this only applies to parents who were married at the time of the child's birth. Unmarried fathers have to get the court's or the mother's agreement to gain parental responsibility. Education legislation defines a parent as anyone who has this parental responsibility or is looking after the child and there is no obligation on schools to release information to anyone without such parental responsibility.

In many cases when we talk about parents we are referring to one, usually the mother. It is often valuable, however, to encourage the active participation of both parents, including step-parents and other partners. Sometimes this may mean a flexibility in service delivery, perhaps to see the family in the evening and/or at home or together on neutral territory. The reasons for promoting a joint approach are not always obvious but nevertheless important. Having a child with SEN puts both individuals and families under pressure. Lack of mutual support and understanding can exacerbate the stresses, to the detriment of everyone. When both parents are actively involved:

- it enables the responsibilities to be shared
- information is less likely to get distorted
- it promotes appropriate expectations
- it helps parents to come to terms with the difficult feelings they may be experiencing
- it can point both parents to sources of information and support
- it helps to maintain a positive relationship for the child with both parents
- it promotes consistency of care for the child.

It is not always easy, nor always appropriate, to actively involve both parents, but where it is not going to be disadvantageous to the child it is worth considering how to promote a joint approach.

Looked after children

Some children, for many reasons, are not living with either of their natural parents. For children with disabilities and SEN this is more likely to be the case than in the rest of the population. For such children, communication may need to be maintained with several adults.

'Looked after' children are either 'accommodated' or are the subject of a care order. The first is a voluntary arrangement between parents and Social Services and is usually the outcome of a request for help. Parents must have the opportunity to be involved in all meetings and decisions about their child.

Where there has been a care order the local authority share parental responsibility with the parents, whether the child is living at home or not. There will be a social worker responsible for the child's welfare and this is the person who should be approached to discuss permission for referrals. He or she should be invited to all major reviews and should ensure that Education is represented at any case conferences arranged by the SSD. The social worker will be able to give information about the continuing rights and responsibilities of the child's natural parents and what is appropriate communication with them.

The child may be cared for either in a children's home or in a foster family. If the child is in residential care, it is helpful to establish a close relationship with the keyworker who can then communicate with other staff in the home. Foster carers may be looking after children on a temporary or more long-term basis. Although they do not have any legal parental responsibility they do take the parental role for children on day-to-day matters and communication needs to be maintained with them in the same way as with other parents.

In some more complex cases, a guardian *ad litem* is appointed by the courts. This person has the responsibility for the oversight of major decisions for a child and will report to the court on the child's needs.

Summary

Partnership with parents requires professionals to be non-judgemental, have a high level of sensitivity and pay attention to processes as well as the content of communication. It requires not only interpersonal skills but also organisational structures and policies which ensure that good practice for SEN and home–school partnership is part of the whole early years ethos.

CHAPTER 5

Joint Planning for Children with Identified Needs

Children who have significant difficulties in one or more areas of their development and have had assessments and probably a home intervention programme, may enter early years education with a good level of information available about their current SEN. For most children there will be a continuing need for ongoing assessment to help clarify the best way forward. Small children are developing quickly and continual assessment and monitoring is important for all children in the early years.

Some children with a high level of complex and/or severe needs may begin their schooling in special provision. A number of these children may stay in a segregated setting throughout their school life. Other children may find themselves in an assessment nursery where there is often a high level of staff expertise. Increasingly, however, parents are seeking mainstream provision for their children where they can play and learn alongside their peers. This is especially so in the early years.

There is some debate about whether intensive specialist provision early on will give some children skills to enhance their longer-term inclusion or whether children should be first given an opportunity to learn and play alongside their peers. What is agreed, however, is that all staff should have a good knowledge of the child's needs which enables appropriate approaches and expectations to be made.

Although the law now says that admission policies must not discriminate against children with SEN, the response parents receive when they approach a school or nursery may not be particularly favourable. It will depend on the ethos and value system of the school, the organisational structure and the level of confidence that staff have in being able to meet the child's needs. In some schools, normal functioning is stressed and any different or additional needs are taken in their stride. Where mainstream schools are less than welcoming there may be a fear that the child will take up a disproportionate amount of time and attention, and that support services will not be available.

In some hard-pressed LEAs, resources are certainly stretched to the limit, but even here some schools are much more accepting than others, and more prepared to develop their knowledge, skills and structures to meet the needs of all their pupils as individuals. Inclusive education is a process, both for the child and for the school. There are always improvements to be made, whatever the starting point.

Factors which support inclusive practices

Judy Sebba and Darshan Sachdev (1997) have collated studies that have evaluated practice in inclusive education. Among the factors they have identified which promote inclusive education are:

- the quality of joint planning – especially in relation to the effective use of support in the classroom
- educational labels rather than categorical labels, e.g. reading difficulty rather than Down's Syndrome
- teachers who provide a role model for pupils in terms of their expectations and the respect and value they demonstrate for all pupils
- strategies which raise children's skills in communicating; some children do not cue in to more subtle communications
- teaching strategies which enable all pupils to participate and learn
- pupil participation and learning which can be enhanced by high expectations, drawing on pupils' previous experiences and maximising peer support
- flexible use of support which enhances rather than impedes the process of inclusive education.

Meeting the child and parents

Before any planning takes place it is very helpful for the teachers who will be most involved to have met with the child and her parents. Talking about someone who has become a real person is much more meaningful than having just a name. Even if it raises anxieties about how to meet needs, it will help to specify those needs in the context of the whole child rather than as abstract concepts.

Joint planning meeting

The rest of this chapter is intended to help people think through the needs of individual children and how these can be met in the classroom and beyond. The importance of this initial meeting in school or nursery cannot be over-emphasised for the following reasons:

- gathering and sharing all relevant information
- enabling good quality planning to take place
- handing over between professionals
- valuing the contributions that everyone makes
- establishing good communications
- establishing positive relationships
- promoting a positive 'can-do' ethos
- reassuring parents
- reassuring and supporting staff who will be in direct contact with the child
- addressing potential difficulties early on
- detailing the need for any specific resources from outside school/nursery.

Many parents, especially those who are on their own, appreciate being given the opportunity to bring a friend or other supporter along with them. It not only gives them more confidence, but they are able to talk over afterwards what has been said in the meeting. Parents of children with significant needs should already have been informed of any voluntary agency who may be able to support them and also about the Named Person or Independent Parental Supporter. It is a good idea to check that they do have this information.

Professionals are likely to know each other as colleagues and need to be aware of doing anything that may make parents feel excluded. This includes discussing another matter in their hearing, or using first names when the family are not offered the same option.

There will be a lot to discuss and detailed plans to be made. It is essential that enough time be given for this, although some of the basic information gathering could be done beforehand. It is useful to use a form, such as that shown in Figure 5.1, detailing contact information for those who should attend a joint planning meeting. The agenda of the meeting will need to include gathering of information, general planning, developing an IEP that identifies short-term targets for the child and dates for review.

The participants in the meeting will have the following contributions to make.

Parents will know:

- their child's history
- their child's personality
- what she can currently do at home and what she is just beginning to learn
- whether she is able to settle to one activity or flits from one thing to another
- what she particularly likes to do and/or is good at
- what activities she is not interested in or actively resists
- how determined, confident or dependent she is
- the experiences she has already had and her responses to these experiences
- what encourages, upsets and soothes her
- the circumstances in which she is most and least cooperative
- the circumstances in which she is most anxious or most confident
- other things that influence her mood and motivation
- how she communicates
- how she deals with frustration
- what they have found has worked well in supporting their child to learn.

Parents will be able to give their child's views about things. Even when children do not have language they are capable of communicating likes and dislikes, preferences and anxieties.

Parents will also know about specific circumstances at home and at work that will impinge on their own involvement. Parents may be reluctant to appear uncooperative or to divulge what they see as personal facts and may therefore agree to participate in actions which they are unlikely to be able to carry through. This sets up bad feelings all round. Great care needs to be taken to ensure that decisions are made together and not imposed.

Parents are likely to be concerned about how happy their child will be in school, how she will settle in, how she will manage and learn, whether or not she will be able to make friends and what will happen at playtime. Many parents will be very aware of their young child's vulnerabilities and will be especially protective.

Teachers/nursery officers will share some of the knowledge that is brought to the meeting by parents and other professionals. Their specific expertise, however, lies in knowledge of:

- the developmental needs of this age group
- the educational value of play and other activities for young children
- a range of teaching methods and approaches
- the structure of the day and the week – what happens and when
- the curriculum that is on offer
- what children need in order to carry out certain activities
- the available resources
- expectations for work and behaviour
- the layout of the school – classroom, playground, big halls and corridors
- policies and procedures for a variety of issues
- roles and responsibilities within the school or nursery.

Teachers are likely to be concerned about helping the child make progress, whether they will have the time and resources to do this effectively, where their support is coming from, how this child's needs will affect their ability to manage the needs of the rest of the class and the expectations on them from parents and others.

EPs will know:

- about the interaction between different areas of child development
- what is within the range of normal functioning and what gives rise to concern
- what is needed to develop and maintain a child's confidence, self-esteem and motivation
- factors within an organisation which help to promote communication and a positive ethos
- factors within classrooms which enhance social interaction
- about learning styles
- ways of modifying the curriculum and adapting the environment
- ways of looking at and managing difficult behaviour
- about relevant legislation and special needs procedures within the LEA
- the range of available resources within the LEA, access procedures and criteria
- about any support groups in the locality.

EPs are likely to be concerned that the child is seen as a whole person, not only in terms of her difficulties in accessing the curriculum. They will focus on all the interactive factors within the context of the classroom, the school and the family to ensure that these are taken into account when addressing needs. They will be particularly concerned that everyone has appropriate expectations.

Health professionals will know:

- the child's medical history and identified health-related difficulties
- the implications these may have for learning and development
- any other implications they may have
- what specific health-related interventions have been undertaken and/or may be necessary
- any specialist equipment that may be necessary
- available resources and how to access these
- what monitoring is required
- their own organisational structures in relation to communication with others
- about any relevant voluntary agencies
- what training they are able to offer.

Some health professionals may also have detailed knowledge of the family's medical and social history.

Health professionals are likely to be most focused on ensuring that the child makes optimum progress in their specific area of concern. They may want to know how programmes that they devise and strategies they suggest will be put in place by those in regular contact with the child. Where health workers cannot attend a meeting in person, it is helpful to request written reports from them well in advance. These should give details of their past and future involvement and outline the implications that the child's needs have for their learning. Suggestions for adaptations and/or specific interventions would also be welcome.

Specific areas of Special Educational Need

Each of the following sections deals with a specific SEN. They are structured to assist early years staff and others find out what they need to know in order to plan for the child to have an optimum pre-school and infant school experience. This means ensuring that they have access to the activities on offer and that there are frameworks in place to facilitate social inclusion.

Many children with special needs have multiple disability. For these children early years workers will want to know the answers to questions in several sections. Likewise not all the questions in each section will be appropriate. It may be a good idea to think about what information is needed before the first planning meeting using the checklists provided in this chapter.

Be precise in asking for extra help where necessary

When additional help is to be sought from the LEA, it is useful if schools are precise about how they are utilising their own resources and what they need in addition to these. Asking for support for specific interventions is better than simply asking for someone to be available for so many hours. One of the main criticisms of special needs support is that it is often unfocused and assistants are not always clear about their exact function other than 'being with' the child in question. The focus needs to be on what is necessary for the child to have access to the full learning environment.

Don't panic!

These lists of questions may look very daunting and may make a teacher or nursery officer feel that the task of working with a child with SEN will be overwhelming. The reality is that knowledge can be quite freeing. Understanding more precisely what is required and planning how needs can be met raises confidence. Panic is more likely to set in when people are at a loss to know what to do and have to think on their feet all the time. Planning at the outset how all the adults in the class or group as well as the other children can be involved is a way of reducing stress.

Physical needs

Physical needs could involve difficulties with mobility, with manipulation or with the processes that affect language or bodily functions such as eating or toileting. Communication and self-help skills are discussed later in this chapter so this section is restricted to issues that affect mobility and manipulation. The multidisciplinary meeting should include a physiotherapist and where possible an OT. Where communication or eating is an issue, a SLT should also be present.

Some children have a physical difficulty as the result of an accident or illness. Others will have conditions such as cerebral palsy or spina bifida. Children who have little control over their physical bodies, including their ability to communicate, may have very alert and able minds. Others may have a learning difficulty in addition to their physical disability.

The law now says that all new schools should be built so that all children can have access. The interventions that are planned will depend both on the answers to the questions below and the present environment and resources of the school.

What you need to know

The child's level of independent mobility:

- how well he is able to move without assistance and with assistance
- what sort of assistance is required?
- the child's ability and willingness to communicate his need for assistance
- circumstances in which extra support may be required, e.g. steps, sloping or uneven surfaces
- the child's confidence in getting around on his own
- the sorts of things which might promote his confidence
- does he need additional time to get from place to place?

Is he likely to be vulnerable in the playground? in what ways?

- What might make him less vulnerable?
- Are there any activities that cannot be adapted for him?
- What should happen at these times?
- Is any physical activity particularly stressful?
- What helps to make it less stressful?

Does he get very tired at certain times?

- What is the best way of dealing with this? What happens at home?
- Would arrangements need to be made for him to have a nap at school?

Are there any activities that he particularly enjoys or is good at?

What are the best sitting arrangements?

- If the child has a wheelchair what help does he need to get in and out of it?
- Is there a need for special seating in the classroom?
- How is that arranged and what should happen when the child begins to outgrow this?
- Does he need anything else to maintain a posture that enables him to participate in tabletop or other activities.

Does the child have a difficulty maintaining his balance?

- What assistance does he need with this?
- Does the child have control over his movements, e.g. does he fling his arms out?
- What is the best way of making sure that other children can play with him but avoid flailing arms? What happens at home?

Does the child have a particular strength/weakness in one side?

• What does this mean for presenting activities?

What level of control does he have over the manipulation of objects?

• What helps him to manipulate things better?
• What factors in posture and physical support make a difference?
• What things does he particularly like to play with?
• Is there anything that other children need to know/do to be able to play with him?

Does he need exercises to be carried out at school? How often, how long for?

• Who is the most appropriate person to do this?
• What training is needed for staff?
• Who will carry this out and when?

Does he need any equipment?

• Who will monitor and maintain this?

What interventions have taken place so far and with what outcome?

Are there communication or self-help needs? If so, move on to the appropriate sections.

Self-help needs

Feeding, toileting and dressing are skills that small children are still developing and not all children entering nursery or school are fully independent. It is also not uncommon for children to regress in their abilities when they have had changes or stresses in their lives. Independence skills, especially toileting, often give rise to strong opinions, feelings and potential conflict. In infant schools especially, it appears to cause busy teachers most concern and anxiety. The health visitor and/or the EP will be able to give information about these needs – if the child has difficulty eating then the SLT can also provide advice.

Feeding: What you need to know

• To what extent is the child able to feed herself independently?
• Is she motivated to try to feed herself?
• Does she have any oral motor difficulties, i.e. can she bite, chew, suck and swallow?
• If so, what interventions have been in place to address this?

- Does her food have to be of a particular consistency?
- How does she get food from plate to mouth?
- What help, if any, does she need with drinks?
- Is she independent but very messy? What can be done to alleviate this problem?
- Is she independent but very slow?
- Is it appropriate for extra time to be made available? How can this be arranged?
- Does the child have strong likes and dislikes for certain foods?
- Are mealtimes a source of potential conflict?
- What in particular might trigger this off?
- What alleviates this?
- Are there medical concerns about diet, e.g. is the child failing to thrive, very listless or potentially lacking essential nutrients?
- If so, has the advice of a dietitian been sought?

Toileting: What you need to know

- Does the child have a physical difficulty with his bladder or bowels that means that he is unlikely ever to be clean and/or dry?
- Has the child developed skills that have since been lost?
- Is any possible reason for this known and is it a continuing concern?
- If the child is in nappies how long do they stay dry/clean?
- Does the child indicate when he has soiled/wet himself – how?
- Is he distressed by having a soiled or wet nappy?
- Is he able to indicate the urge to empty his bladder or bowels? How?
- Does he have any level of control over his bladder and/or bowels, i.e. can he 'hold on' for any length of time?
- Is there any pattern to his toileting habits, e.g. needing to go 30 minutes after a meal?
- What do parents currently do at home?
- Does the child use a potty/a child-sized toilet seat?
- What encourages the child to get on and stay put?
- What is considered a reasonable time for the child to sit on a potty or toilet?
- Has there been any attempt at toilet training?
- What was the outcome?
- Is there a need to develop a home–school programme?
- What are the child's present expectations about being changed and washed?
- What resources and facilities are available at school?

Dressing: What you need to know

- To what extent can the child dress/undress herself independently?
- Is she motivated to do things for herself?
- What are the expectations at home?
- Can she manage but is very slow?
- Is this a potential source of conflict?
- What alleviates/exacerbates this?
- Which circumstances in school will require the child to dress herself?
- What exactly will she need help with?
- Is there a need to allow extra time?
- What are the expectations on other children to help each other?
- What are the expectations to try to do things independently before asking for help?
- Is it possible to have clothes that are easier to manage, e.g. velcro fastenings on shoes?

Communication needs

It is estimated that as many as one in five children entering school have communication difficulties for one reason or another. Although specific programmes can be developed for individuals, a strong focus on language development for all children in the early years is essential as this underpins many other areas of development, especially thinking skills and social interaction.

The person most involved will be the SLT. If the child has a social and communication difficulty on the autistic spectrum, the EP will also need to be involved. The child and his family may already have seen these professionals but this is not always the case.

What you need to know

Does the child have a hearing loss? If so, please also see the section on hearing impairment.

Are the child's skills delayed in all or most areas of development?

- Is his language at the same level? If so, please also see the section on learning difficulties.

Is English the child's first language?

- If not, does the child have difficulties in understanding or using the language he hears at home?

• If the child's skills are age appropriate in their own language then they do not have a special need in language development. Many of the interventions for children with language difficulties or delay are, however, also helpful for children learning an additional language.

What is the nature of the child's difficulty with communication?

• Is language normal but delayed or is it disordered in some way?
• Is the communication difficulty part of a wider social difficulty?
• Is the communication causing frustration and challenging behaviour?

Ongoing assessment may be necessary to identify the child's specific difficulties.

Motivation and participation

To what extent is the child motivated to communicate:

• with adults?
• with other children?

Which circumstances/individuals promote this motivation?
Which circumstances, if any, inhibit communication and need to be avoided?
How does the child respond when others make approaches?

• adults
• other children.

To what extent does the child:

• follow routines?
• join in structured activities?
• play meaningfully with other children?

What would be initial steps to support the child's participation?

Receptive skills/understanding

To what extent is the child able to listen?
What are the best ways of gaining the child's attention:

• individually
• in a group?

What is known to be useful in supporting the child's understanding?
Has the child any knowledge of sign language?

• If so which signs are in use?
• Are there any training implications for staff (and other children)?

How much information can the child understand at a time:

- one idea
- more?

What are good ways of checking that the child has understood?

Expressive communication

Does the child have a problem with:

- saying words clearly
- word-finding
- sentence construction?

Does the child initiate interaction with adults/with other children?

- How do they do this?
- How successful are these attempts – with what outcome?
- What are the best ways of responding to the child's attempts to communicate?

How does the child communicate:

- needs
- ideas
- feelings?

Are there words/phrases that can be interpreted by the family but are difficult for unfamiliar people to understand? How can this knowledge be transferred?

What, if anything, does the child use to augment verbal interaction?

What could be encouraged and developed?

What would be helpful for other children to know or learn to optimise communication with this particular child?

What affects the child's level of frustration and how is this frustration expressed?

Which ways of managing this have had some success?

Which communication targets would best help settle the child into the school or nursery?

Hearing needs

Many small children under seven years of age experience conductive hearing loss at some time or another, especially when they have a cold. When a fairly severe hearing difficulty has been identified prior to school it is more likely to be a sensory-neural loss which may be permanent.

Severe and/or frequent conductive loss, however, can affect a child's language and social development, and needs to be taken seriously. In many cases a child with a sensory-neural hearing impairment can have their residual hearing affected by an additional fluctuating conductive loss.

The audiologist and the peripatetic teacher for the hearing impaired will be able to answer many queries about a child who cannot hear well.

Please also see the section above on communication difficulties.

What you need to know

What is the nature of the child's difficulties?

- Does the child have more residual hearing in one ear? Which one?
- What sort of sounds can the child hear and at what level?
- Does the child have a history of fluctuating hearing?
- Under which circumstances is hearing worse or better?
- What does this mean for the child receiving instruction in the classroom?
- Where does the teacher need to be in relation to the child?
- What does this mean for less formal situations?

How well can the child lip-read?
What makes this easier?
Is the child used to hearing aids?

- Are there any difficulties with these?
- Has the child developed any skills in managing these independently?
- How are hearing aids monitored?

Does the child use any signing to support communication?
If so, are there any training implications?
Are there circumstances in which poor hearing puts the child at risk?
How can these risks be addressed?
Has the child had experience of playing with other children?
What helps to make this successful?
How well has the child adapted to these difficulties?
What helps the child make progress?
Are there situations or circumstances that the child finds particularly distressing?
What helps?
Which activities might need specific adaptations or arrangements, e.g. music and singing?
What early years input has the child and family already received?
What are the outcomes from this?

Visual needs

Comparatively few young children born in the UK have severe problems with their eyesight. Teachers are therefore less used to making adaptations for them than they may be, for instance, for a child with a hearing loss. There are many reasons why a child has poor vision, and specific visual impairments may require different adaptations in the classroom. The peripatetic teacher for the visually impaired will be helpful in identifying appropriate responses. Some children will be registered on the BD8 – the register for the blind and partially sighted. Opthalmologists make the decision about eligibility but it is the parent's decision to register.

What you need to know

What is the nature of the child's visual impairment?

What are the expected outcomes for this child – will his eyesight change in any way over time?

How much does he currently see, in which ways and under which conditions?

How has the child responded/adapted to his specific visual difficulties and the use of his residual vision?

What compensatory skills will the child need to develop?

What are the implications for movement around the class and school?

What implication does the above have for learning:

- in the presentation of tabletop activities
- in the lighting required
- in the size of lettering required
- in participating in physical activities
- in creative play – painting, modelling etc.
- in imaginative play – home-corner, miniature people
- using construction toys
- using computers
- at carpet time
- for stories and reading?

What can be done to help the child integrate learning so that experiences become part of a whole rather than fragmented?

Are there any specific difficulties that need to be addressed in unstructured times either in the class or outside?

How much experience does the child have in playing with other children?

What do other children need to know and do in order to facilitate the child's participation?

Does the child wear glasses?

Are there implications for the use and care of these?

What arrangements need to be in place for mobility training?

General learning needs

Several of the other difficulties described in this chapter will also apply to the child who has an overall learning difficulty, in particular those to do with communication and behaviour. A child who has a developmental delay in cognitive skills is also likely to behave like a much younger child. The greatest difficulty for those working in an early years setting is that young children are often strongly self-directed and within an educational establishment they are often required to follow directions. Some do this quite happily and others are more resistant. Finding an appropriate balance that allows for freedom of choice but extends learning challenges the skills of early years teachers.

Those children who have had, or who are having, an emotionally distressing time may also find it difficult to concentrate, learn, remember, problem solve or play happily with other children.

What you need to know

What are the child's learning styles? Which are being used most:

- watching and copying
- physical – needs to engage the whole body much of the time
- experimental – seeing what happens
- creative/problem solving – making up stories, symbolic play
- listening, asking questions?

What is helpful in maintaining concentration:

- type of activity – which?
- doing things with adults/children
- time of day?

Is there anything that is particularly distracting for the child?

What does the child enjoy doing?

What interest could link in with activities, e.g. animals, a new baby, football?

What else stimulates the child's motivation?

In which circumstances does the child appear to learn best?

Following directions

What supports the child in following directions:

- gaining visual attention – ensuring they are looking at the speaker
- using their name
- standing close to them
- making directions short and simple (but grammatically correct)
- checking understanding
- praising people next to them for following instructions
- praising them for part-compliance
- starting something with them
- reminding and reinforcing
- review and reinforcement (telling them what they have done well)?

Being independent

Will the child do things independently or need encouragement to try?
Are new activities resisted – what helps in introducing different things?
Does the child repeat known activities over and over again?
Does the child need to know that it is acceptable to make mistakes?
Does the child need 'larger than life' praise?
What have parents found most useful in helping their child to learn?
What are the learning priorities for the child?
What are they presently able to do and what needs to happen next?

Emotional, social and behavioural needs

Structured situations are not suited to all small children. Sometimes a child is said to have a behaviour difficulty where, in fact, expectations are inappropriate for their age or developmental stage. Many small children require a high level of physical activity, a variety of activities, opportunities to stand and watch without doing anything active at all and plenty of time to play, develop imaginative skills and problem solve in make-believe situations.

Other children demand a lot of adult attention, which is not easy or appropriate to provide. Sometimes these children have learnt that they can gain attention by behaving in ways it is difficult to ignore. They need to learn to gain attention by positive behaviours.

Some behaviours cluster together and may indicate that the child may be on the autistic spectrum. These behaviours include difficulties with:

- social interaction
- communication
- imagination.

These are usually associated with rigid, repetitive patterns of behaviour and often a fear of unfamiliar situations.

Children who are very unhappy are particularly worrying for teachers or nursery officers, either because they express anger indiscriminately and other children get hurt or because they withdraw from interaction. Some of these children may have experienced abuse, rejection or loss that affects their views of themselves and other people. Other children have simply not learnt the skills they need to cooperate positively with other people and these have to be taught.

Finding out

The most important thing is not to jump to conclusions about why a child is behaving in a way which is difficult to manage, and work closely with the parent to identify the difficulties and how they can best be addressed. The health visitor and EP will be helpful people to talk to.

What you need to know

Does the child have any other difficulties, e.g. with learning or communication?

What are the exact behaviours that are difficult?
How frequently do they occur?
What are the triggers for these, if any?
Is there any pattern to them?
What do parents say about how the child behaves at home?
Which positive activities does he enjoy doing?
What is known to be effective in encouraging willing cooperation?
What soothes the child and has a calming effect?
What does the child say about the way they feel?
What are priorities for the child to learn?

- about himself and others
- to manage the expression of his feelings
- to establish good interactions with other children
- to follow adult directions
- to settle to an activity.

Medical needs

Children may have a medical need in conjunction with a physical disability or other special need. The majority, however, will have a single condition such as epilepsy or asthma. As such this may not be defined as SEN, but does require staff awareness. In most circumstances, the school nurse or health visitor will be able to provide information and advice.

What you need to know

- The condition that the child has, and any educational implications?
- What should be avoided wherever possible?
- What preventative measures/adaptations are helpful?
- What are the signs of any impending attack?
- What should be the immediate response of staff?
- What should happen next?
- Who should be contacted in the event of an attack at school?
- Does the child need medication to be administered at school?
- Where will this be kept and who will administer this?
- How will records be kept?
- Are there training implications? How can these be arranged?

Outcome of meetings

Teachers may feel at the end of the initial planning meeting that there is an enormous amount to do. When a range of issues are thought through at the beginning, however, it saves much time and anxiety later on. Many of the plans and adaptations that make a great difference to a child and her family may, in fact, be quite small and once they are in place they become routine. It is also useful to discuss at the outset how existing resources can be utilised most effectively and, without being negative, give everyone a sense of what is realistic. It is very helpful to know who is going to be doing what and how everything will be monitored. If something is not quite working as it should then there are plans to review and adapt accordingly. It is worth remembering that it is not only *what* happens that matters but also *how* it happens.

The following checklist (Figure 5.1) can be used to help with initial general planning and also with the IEP that sets short-term targets for the child.

- Are any physical adaptations needed?
- What exactly are these?
- What curricular adaptations need to be made?
- Do any adaptations need to be made to the timetable? What are these?
- Is any additional equipment needed? What will it be used for and who will monitor its use? Where will it be kept when not in use?

What specific support is needed from:

- the class teacher
- in-school support resources
- other children

- parents
- additional LEA resources
- others?

What training needs have been identified?

- Who are appropriate trainers and who will make contact with them?
- Who will be responsible for devising and monitoring the IEP?

What continuing communications will be put in place?

- Who will communicate with whom, when, how often and how?
- In particular, who will be taking responsibility for ongoing communication between home and school? What are the joint expectations for this?
- When is the date of the next home–school meeting?
- When is the date of the next multidisciplinary meeting to review progress and needs?

Summary

The joint planning meeting should aim to reassure parents and teachers alike that there is a coordinated team approach to meeting the child's needs. Everyone should have a good understanding of their own responsibilities and the support that is there to advise and help when necessary. Many of the professionals in the team, however, are visitors rather than working on site. It is how the whole school or nursery community also work together in responding to the child's needs that will make a difference to her happiness and progress in school.

Katharine's experience

Michael, who is now six years old, has a specific language disorder and is attending his local mainstream primary school. His mother, Katharine, is very positive about what is now happening for him and has no doubt about what makes the difference:

It's because there is a Speech and Language Service in Education now. Before, when it was in Health, it was difficult for the speech therapist to come into school, there was no exchange of files and I had to take Michael out of school to the clinic. Now the speech therapist comes into school regularly and talks to the teachers. She is able to train up the classroom assistant. We have joint meetings, and I know that there are people in school who are planning for him. I don't have to pass things on from one person to another and sometimes lose half of it in the passing. Now it's like a weight lifted off me, I don't have to worry about him every day he's in school.

Katharine's experience has not always been so positive. Michael had been a very observant baby and had reached his physical milestones early so it was a real shock to discover at the age of two and a half that all was not well:

He was full of energy, and being quite uncooperative. I would say things to him over and over in different ways and he didn't take much notice. I asked the health visitor for some ideas to help getting him to bed and when she came to visit, she noticed immediately that his language wasn't developing as it should. It was really hard to reconcile in my mind; we had been such proud parents. I needed a lot of reassurance and, although they had to be realistic, I was also looking for people to be positive, too.

Following a developmental check and a referral to the CDC Michael was offered speech and language therapy, first individually and then in a group. Soon after starting school Michael was given some support for two mornings a week. Katharine was pleased with the help that was being given but not happy about other aspects of her involvement with the professionals:

All this time I was trying to find out for myself, trying to get information. No one told me about AFASIC (the Association for all Speech Impaired Children) and we had been going to speech therapy for a year before I knew about the local parents' centre, which is very, very good. It's important for parents to have support, not to feel alone. You worry about what's going to happen for your child, you want the best and you don't know what to do. I found out most of what I know about the Code of Practice stages and Statementing from a friend who has a child with special needs. People did speak to me about it but I was overwhelmed with it all and didn't understand everything. It's hard to ask sometimes, you don't want to appear stupid but at first you just don't know what people are talking about. Parents aren't professionals who talk about these things all the time, they should be spoken to in plain English and step by step. Parents want to be involved and will be able to be involved; information should be offered and given in a way that parents can understand. I can talk their language now but not at the beginning.

HOME, SCHOOL AND AGENCIES CONTACT INFORMATION

Child's name_____ Date of birth_____

HOME INFORMATION

Address_____

_____

Name of parents/carers_____

Contact numbers: At home_____ At work_____

Other carers_____

Contact number and/or address_____

_____

Relatives or friends who may be involved

Name(s)_____

Contact details_____

Language(s) spoken at home_____

Community language interpreter

Name_____

Contact number_____

SCHOOL INFORMATION

Name of school/early years provision_____

Address_____

_____

Telephone number(s)_____

Name of school/nursery keyworker_____

When available for contact_____

Name of SENCO_____

When available for contact_____

Agreements for home–school communication_____

Figure 5.1 Contact information for home, school and agencies – *continued opposite*

Record of information given to parents/carers and how communicated

e.g. special needs policy given in writing and explained in meeting with interpreter

AGENCIES' INFORMATION
General Practitioner

Name_____

Contact number_____

Other medical professionals

Name_____

Role_____

Contact number_____

Name_____

Role_____

Contact number_____

Educational Psychologist

Name_____

Contact number_____

When available for contact_____

Education support agencies

Name_____

Contact number_____

Named LEA Officer

Name_____

Contact number_____

Named Person or other parent supporter

Name_____

Contact number_____

Figure 5.1 Contact information for home, school and agencies – *continued overleaf*

Other support agencies

Name_____

Contact number_____

Social Worker

Name_____

Contact number_____

When available for contact_____

OTHER INFORMATION

Special equipment

Item(s)_____

Provider_____

Contact number_____

Name of person monitoring use_____

Contact number_____

Any medication_____

Purpose_____

Administration details_____

Inter-agency and parent communication agreement:

(What information will be sent out, to whom and what are parents' wishes about this?)

_____

_____

Any other relevant information given by parents/carers to be communicated to those working within the team:_____

_____

Next annual or other Inter-agency review will be held on:

_____

Date form completed:_____

Updated:_____

Figure 5.1 Contact information for home, school and agencies

CHAPTER 6

In-School Communication

Ethos, communication and effective schools

There is increasing acknowledgement that the culture of any organisation is closely linked to its effectiveness. Collaboration and communication are part of the overall ethos and the whole atmosphere of a school or nursery is affected by the extent to which there is collegiality. The schools that are most effective have a culture in which the head teacher has a clear vision of aims but where everyone takes responsibility for meeting organisational goals. Where these goals include promoting high expectations for all children, there will be an incentive to clarify pupil needs, to work together both within the school and with others to raise the achievement of all. Clear lines of communication ensure that this works in practice, information is shared in a regular and accessible way, people know what their responsibilities are and where their support lies. Where individual needs are seen as a priority, time and resources are more likely to be available for planning and review. Where there is an ethos which focuses on possibilities rather than problems there will be a more relaxed and positive view of SEN. Where everyone in mainstream provision takes responsibility for making inclusion work, no one has to face challenges alone.

Talking with others about a child

Discussing children with other staff members can be very supportive. People do need an opportunity to express anxiety or exasperation but communication about children in the staff room is powerful in establishing attitudes and expectations. A negative framework, which focuses exclusively on what the child cannot do or how badly behaved she is, undermines confidence and promotes self-fulfilling labels. Where a positive ethos pervades the culture of an establishment, this includes the way people talk about, as well as to, children and their parents. This includes the front-line administrative staff who are often the first people to meet with parents or talk with them on the 'phone. First impressions of a school or nursery are powerful and school secretaries carry a special responsibility for the messages they convey.

The Special Educational Needs Coordinator

The Special Educational Needs Coordinator (SENCO) has a pivotal role for communication with those both outside and inside school. The responsibilities inherent in this are central to the progress that children make. Although there has been a wide range of practice in different schools, the role and status of SENCOs is being gradually clarified and this process has been assisted by the publication of guidance from the DfEE. Many primary head teachers, feeling unable to fund a SENCO post, have taken on the considerable extra work themselves and struggled to keep abreast of it. Others have recognised the importance of the distinct SENCO role and have made this a priority within their budgets, even if it is only for a few hours a week. Many SENCOs have indeed complained of not having enough time to do the job properly. The knowledge and skills, however, that are now being developed in schools in relation to special needs are largely due to those individuals who have taken on this role with such commitment. Early years provision, now expected to follow the Code of Practice (DfEE 1994), is also obliged to have someone named as the coordinator for special needs.

Clarifying roles and responsibilities

In many schools and nurseries, the SENCO is the first point of contact for professionals and the second point of contact for parents, after the class teacher. In others, there remains a lack of clarity about the distinct roles of the class teacher, head teacher, and the SENCO about responsibility for SEN. This can result in confusion, duplication and bad feeling. Collaboration as a result of policy and planning is good practice – poor communication about who should be doing what is not. It is helpful to work out in advance who meets with parents and when, how outcomes of meetings are communicated to others and the procedures for referrals. Arrangements for providing cover for professionals to meet with key staff can be problematic, and where responsibilities for this are agreed beforehand it ensures that professional time is put to best use.

Head teachers and SENCOs also need to agree who chairs and records major review meetings, how SEN records will be maintained and accessed, who attends case conferences outside school and how training will be coordinated. It is essential that the SENCO and head teacher meet together regularly to clarify the above, share information and monitor SEN practice in the school.

The SENCO and communication

The communication role of the SENCO is crucial in ensuring that there is good collaboration between school, parents and others. Information needs to be disseminated in a meaningful way to all those who are involved with a child. SENCOs need consultative skills as well as special needs knowledge – telling people what to do is rarely as successful as helping to define problems and strategies together.

The communication role of the SENCO will be facilitated by:

- maintaining up-to-date contact information about carers and all professionals involved with a child – their names, addresses and telephone numbers
- discussing reports from professionals with relevant staff in terms of their implications for the child's learning
- arranging annual reviews well in advance and having them in a block of time to facilitate the involvement of a range of agencies
- having an effective filing system so that information on the SEN Register is quickly accessible and can be updated easily; there are now good computer packages available
- making relevant information about the child in the educational setting available to professionals and others (communication is often one-way, which underestimates the vital on going assessment role of key staff)
- facilitating meetings between professionals, and key members of staff – possibly covering classes where necessary
- facilitating home–school partnership between parents and key staff
- being available at a regular time for informal discussions with staff
- taking responsibility for ensuring there is effective liaison with support staff and temporary staff

- maintaining and developing a resource base including
  - examples of good practice
  - training given with dates
  - in-school sources of expertise
  - information about external agencies, voluntary bodies and support groups.
- ensuring that transitions go smoothly by facilitating the exchange of information.

In *The SENCO Guide* (DfEE 1997b), the role of the head teacher and governors is said to be crucial in providing financial and other support to the SENCO, in enabling her to carry out her functions effectively. At a minimum level, this includes easy access to a 'phone, a desk and storage facilities. The time factor is also an issue that needs clarification with the head teacher and governors. *The SENCO Guide* gives several suggestions as to how to make time available and how best to manage it.

The keyworker

Although the SENCO is responsible for overall coordination, it is sometimes useful for the member of staff who has most contact with the child – or perhaps a particularly special relationship with the child and/or parents – to be designated the keyworker. This might be a teacher but could also be a support assistant, welfare officer or nursery nurse. If this happens, the roles of keyworker, SENCO and any other relevant staff must be clarified at the outset, together with decisions about how and when communication takes place.

Clarity, continuity and consistency

Communication with support staff

There are different kinds of support staff who may be involved with a child with SEN. If the child is at Stage 2 (school support) then they may be receiving some additional help from someone in school. If they are at Stage 3 (school support plus) or Statemented, then the LEA may be funding additional support. This may be support by a teacher or by a non-teaching assistant and could be someone coming in from an outside service. In some LEAs, it is common practice for support service teachers to liaise with the school in determining the role of the special needs assistant and to monitor this support rather than be directly involved themselves.

The relationship between a class teacher and a support assistant can be complex. The following questions may be helpful in clarifying roles and responsibilities.

- How often will the support assistant be in the classroom?
- How will exact days and times be negotiated?
- What is the support assistant there to do?
- How does this fit in with the child's IEP?
- What is the role of the class teacher in the IEP?
- Who decides the day-to-day role of the support assistant?
- What should be the balance between individual work and group work?
- How will the child's inclusion into the class be supported by the assistant?
- Will the support assistant be spending time out of the classroom? How often, and what is the explicit purpose for this?
- What happens when the assistant is not there at the agreed times, e.g. on sick leave or on a course?
- What liaison time needs to be made available for the class teacher and the support assistant to meet together? When will this be?
- How often should regular meetings with parents, the SENCO, the class teacher and the support assistant take place? Who will arrange this?

Communication with lunchtime supervisors

Many children flourish within the classroom, where there is good information about their needs and how best to meet these. It is in the unstructured times of the day when difficulties often arise, particularly at lunchtime. When children have had an unhappy experience during the dinner break, they may bring negative emotions back into the classroom in the afternoon. This does not help anybody. The adults supervising activities in the dining hall or the playground may not be aware of children's specific needs, what it is appropriate to expect from them, helpful approaches to adopt and how they can facilitate social interaction. Both information and skills are needed.

Possible approaches include:

- following agreement with parents, children's individual needs could be discussed with lunchtime supervisors
- the link between behaviour and SEN should be made explicit, together with appropriate responses
- additional training should be provided where necessary.

Tight budgets and contract specifications might mitigate against this good practice but there are ways around this. Here are some of them:

- senior staff provide occasional lunchtime supervision to enable supervisors to have training at this time
- when there is a training day for staff, the lunchtime supervisors routinely have their own training programme; other arrangements are made for staff lunch; money may be available for providing whole or half day training from Standards Funds and other special arrangements
- there is a keyworker lunchtime supervisor for individual children who links with the keyworker teacher or SENCO and then passes on information to colleagues on the child's needs and how to respond to these
- each class or nursery group links with one supervisor so that he or she gets to know the children and the teacher – the children are formally handed over by the teacher to the supervisor at lunchtime; this both enhances status for the supervisor and enables the two members of staff to work more closely together
- training happens 'on-site' with trainers modelling inclusive activities with staff.

Communication with supply teachers

Some of the best practice may be put at risk by a supply teacher not being aware of a child's specific needs. Supply teachers may arrive at a moment's notice with little time to give them information. It is useful, therefore, to plan for this contingency in advance. The SENCO and the class teacher can take responsibility together for planning, with the SENCO ensuring that the information is with the supply teacher as soon as possible: it's not much use if it stays in the desk drawer. Where to find this information could be part of a whole–school or nursery pack for supply staff.

The information must be brief and to the point – no teacher coming into a class will have time to read a file! It may be useful to have just one piece of laminated card with four or five points on it, e.g.: Figure 6.1.

SEN information for supply teachers

JAMES (STATEMENTED) has a hearing difficulty – keep him in the front at carpet time, make sure he is looking directly at you. His left ear has better residual hearing.

CARLO (STAGE 3) has support from the behaviour support team on Tuesdays and Fridays. He responds best to a calm, but firm approach. If he throws a tantrum, the other children know to leave him to get over it – if he goes on for longer than 20 minutes ask a member of staff to take him to the office. A raised voice makes him much worse.

DELLA (STAGE 4) has physiotherapy exercises at lunchtime, just needs reminding to go to the medical room before she has her dinner.

SAMI (STAGE 1) is a new arrival, speaks very little English and is very passive, (learning difficulties?) The class are taking it in turns to play with her. They will be able to tell you who it is this week.

Figure 6.1 SEN information for supply teachers

Continuity

The best laid plans within a school or nursery can be thrown into disarray by a change in personnel. Sometimes there is no chance to prepare for this. If the communication in the school or nursery is good and several people have knowledge of and positive relationships with the children with SEN then this will minimise any negative effects. The SENCO, however, should take responsibility for:

- communication with the member of staff who is 'taking over', however temporarily
- arranging a meeting between this person and any support staff as soon as possible
- communicating with the parents about any interim arrangements
- communicating with the children about the situation in order to reduce any anxiety
- reinforcing peer group support.

Keeping in touch

Sometimes children with SEN have many treatments or illnesses that mean they either are often absent from school or have intermittent long periods of absence. Keeping in touch with such children and their parents maintains good relationships and continuity. A weekly 'phone call is usually welcome, and arrangements for children to make contact is also valuable. This could be in the form of cards or pictures as well as visits. Giving parents some ideas about curriculum-based activities helps to keep the child linked in with what is going on at school.

Child protection

It is sadly the case that children with disabilities and SEN are particularly vulnerable to abuse. All those working with such children need to be aware of this and maintain an appropriate vigilance. Should emotional, physical, or sexual abuse, serious or persistent neglect be suspected, careful monitoring needs to take place. Collated evidence should record incidents with dates, verbatim comments giving rise to concern, and anything else that is worrying. Each school should have a designated teacher responsible for child protection and each LEA will have published procedural guidelines. Teachers who think they have cause to be concerned need to have a three-way meeting with the designated teacher and SENCO to decide on a course of action. This discussion should determine whether a referral to Social Services will be made at this point. Some Social Services Departments (SSDs) have regular drop in sessions for teachers and others working with children, which provide advice and guidance. It is important to maintain positive relationships with parents as much as possible but it should always be made clear that teachers are obliged to follow up concerns and report any disclosures. As this may potentially cause conflict, any referral should be seen to be made by the school, not by any individual.

Communication with other children and other parents

Communication with other children

Young children do not have the same stereotypes and expectations as older children and adults. They are often able to give children with SEN an experience of acceptance that may put others to shame. They will, however, ask questions and be interested in why their classmate is different. There are a number of ways to address these issues. It is valuable to discuss with parents very early on what you might do. Some parents would be very reluctant to draw attention to their child's difficulties and differences. Others are happy for these to be discussed openly. Often children will be able to say for themselves what they would like to happen and how much they want to be part of this.

Ideas for communicating SEN issues with children

With parents' agreement, talk to the class or group about similarities and differences, beginning with the class itself; e.g. some have fair hair, some have dark hair. Then talk about other differences that might mean that children need something extra, e.g. some children do not see as well as others and need glasses. Teachers may then choose to introduce the needs of the child in question.

There are now many books available (some are listed in Appendix 2) which introduce more difficult topics to young children in story form. Reading and discussing these will help to raise issues and answer questions.

Adults with a range of disabilities (but who also have skills in interacting with young children) could be asked to come and talk with children who can then be encouraged to ask questions. Voluntary agencies may be able to put schools and nurseries in touch with people.

Some organisations can provide videos or even live drama groups to raise issues. When given by experienced and sensitive trainers an experiential session can have a very positive impact on attitudes and understanding. This entails replicating some of the experiences that a child with difficulties (usually sensory) may have and what they need to do in their daily lives to adapt to these. This is also very useful for adults!

Sometimes children themselves may choose to tell their story to others and enjoy being the centre of attention. Again, any such proposal should not go ahead without parental agreement.

Communication with other parents

Communication on SEN issues needs to be part of the information that is given out to all parents when children begin school or nursery. An allusion to the school's philosophy on SEN may be useful even earlier, when parents first register their child or even when they make initial enquiries. Written information needs to:

- state the school's SEN policy in understandable language
- outline the commitment to inclusive and anti-discriminatory practices and what this may mean
- clarify how the curriculum on offer will promote the skills of all
- state the school's policy on behaviour including preventative approaches and sanctions
- indicate lines of communication open to parents when they have a concern.

Conflict between parents can, at times, flare up in the playground, often over children's behaviour. Schools may be reluctant to address this directly with individuals but do need to communicate again the appropriate channels for raising issues of concern.

Transitions

Changes often come about because children grow older and move on. These transition periods are potentially difficult, and communication between people at these times makes a great deal of difference to the level of continuity and the smoothness with which transitions occur. People need to be aware that a settling-in period is necessary for both the teacher and the child as they get used to each other.

Between classes

This is usually not so dramatic a change as that between schools. The buildings and staff are familiar and, equally importantly, so are the other children. The overriding need is for good communication with the person who is taking on the major responsibility for the child, usually the class teacher. Ideally, a four-way meeting between the parent, the outgoing teacher, the incoming teacher and the SENCO will provide the following:

- basic information about the child and her SEN
- awareness of any specific vulnerability
- awareness of strengths and any special interests
- information about others involved
- appropriate approaches, adaptations and any specialist equipment
- recent programmes and reviews
- the progress the child has made on past and current targets
- priorities for targets in the immediate future
- arrangements for liaison with parents
- any other essential information, such as other carers, language issues etc.

If a support teacher or special needs assistant has been involved, they should also attend this in-school meeting. A few 'visits' to the teacher, perhaps with a friend, before the new term starts, may also help with this process.

Between schools

Transition between nursery school and infant school or infants and juniors can be a time of anxiety for teachers, parents and children. Again, it is a question of reassurance and putting the right communications in place at the outset.

The following strategies have met with a level of success; the more of them it is possible to put into place the better.

- The SENCO of the new provision attends a review where the child is presently placed to gain as much information as possible and to meet with the parents.
- The 'old' SENCO opens a file that gives all contact details, desirable outcome or other relevant measurements, copies of IEPs, a statement of SEN if applicable, and examples of the child's work over time.
- The SENCO shares this information with the child's new teacher(s).
- The new class teacher visits the child in their nursery or infant setting for a morning or afternoon, discusses her progress with staff and ways in which they have dealt with any difficulties.
- The child is given an opportunity to visit their new school, perhaps accompanied by support staff.
- A planning meeting happens prior to intake with parents and as many professionals as possible (see Chapter 5). This could be combined with the final review held in the old provision.

Case study

Hilda, a child with Down's Syndrome, was due to transfer in September, from her infant class to a junior school the other side of the borough. She had done well in her infant school and had been very settled there. Everyone was anxious about the move. During her annual review in March, which the SENCO of the new school was able to attend, it was suggested that maybe a series of visits in the summer term would help with the transition. Hilda had a special needs assistant four mornings a week so it was decided that she would accompany her to her new school for one morning a week for the second half of the summer term. Hilda really enjoyed this and over the seven visits became familiar with the staff, found out how to get around the school and sat in on some lessons with the person who was to be her new teacher. The teacher's worries about being able to meet Hilda's needs were addressed and she became more confident about the expectations that would be placed on her. The new teacher also met with Hilda's parents and established a rapport with them. When Hilda finally transferred in September she was one step ahead of the other children entering the school for the first time and able to 'show them the ropes'. This raised her status and boosted her self-esteem.

The child who arrives mid-term

Sometimes a child arrives in a class with little or no information and within a short while appears to be having difficulties. Chapter 4 suggests ways of approaching parents, but it may be that the child is in this situation because of disruptions in their home life. Many families in temporary accommodation are moved from one area to another before they finally settle. Some mothers may be escaping a violent situation and be very wary of giving out any information. A sensitivity to these issues is necessary but, where parents are agreeable, making contact with any previous educational provision or professionals is likely to be helpful. If it is the case that the child has been on waiting lists for services in other areas then this might be communicated to current services so that she might receive some priority attention.

Children who leave to go on to other schools

Likewise, when a child moves into another area it is valuable if parental permission is sought to transfer information. Offering the SENCO of a new school or nursery an early telephone conversation might help the child to settle in more quickly and have appropriate provision made for her. An educational social worker (ESW) (also known as educational welfare officer) might be involved if the child disappears without any information being given, especially if she is of school age.

Summary

The effectiveness of in-school communication makes a great deal of difference to children's happiness and progress in school. It is not only the SENCO and teachers who are critical in establishing a positive framework but all those who are connected with the school and who come into contact with the child and her parents.

CHAPTER 7

Issues Affecting Collaboration

The first section of this chapter raises some of the structural and organisational issues involved in developing collaborative practices. The second addresses some of the interpersonal issues that impinge on the success of working relationships.

Structural and organisational issues

Working together – from the top down

There are exhortations everywhere for services and professionals to work together in a spirit of collaboration for the benefit of children and their parents. All over the country there are examples of this happening – but in general it is still piecemeal and fragmented. Often, this 'joined up thinking' is against the odds and due to the determination of individuals rather than the organisational structures in which people work. Early years partnerships are a real attempt to move in the right direction.

There are a number of factors that will influence whether collaboration and coordination become routine and a reality nation-wide. These include:

- government incentives for collaborative practice
- effective liaison between government departments to ensure that the many plans that they are demanding from public services interconnect and support clarity rather than confusion for people in their daily working lives
- understanding by local politicians that joint funding for inter-agency work requires both vision and determination to change present practices, is beneficial to children and their families and is cost-effective in the long run

- liaison between chief executives of local authorities and Health Service managers to develop frameworks for setting joint priorities and joint planning to meet objectives
- commitment from senior managers to work together at the highest level. Within local authorities this means that protection of individual budgets should be secondary to the development of inter-agency client centred practices
- professionals, and professional bodies, who focus on working together rather than defending their particular corner of expertise
- the development of a culture in which inter-agency communication and understanding is given high priority and seen as an effective use of time
- initial training and professional development that clarifies the contexts in which different people work and the perspectives that inform their actions
- joint training and the development of services that provide a 'multidisciplinary team' approach to meeting needs
- the appointment of personnel whose job description includes a liaison role with other agencies and dissemination of relevant information.

Without the senior organisational and professional will and commitment implied in the above, collaborative working will continue to depend on those individuals who are determined to make it happen in their specific contexts. When they leave, collaboration may cease.

Breaking down barriers in Gloucestershire

Gloucestershire is committed to the development of a more coordinated and collaborative service for families and children with SEN. When a three-year review of Children's Services highlighted a lack of consistency the Education committee of the council had a fresh look at how they could build on their existing good practice to offer more integrated provision. They are supported in this by a parents' initiative called *Breaking Down the Barriers*. Among their many activities this group held conferences attended by both Education officers and Social Services managers.   Parents wanted to explain what having a child with SEN meant to them and what it was that they needed.

The council has a joint strategy group looking at Primary Health Care, Housing, Education and Social Services. Managers and fund holders work together on this group to develop good collaborative practice from the top down. An example of this has been the three-way funding of an Early Years Development Officer. Along with providing speech and language centres attached to mainstream schools the LEA is currently funding two speech and language projects in mainstream primary schools. There are already family centres on school sites that potentially give access to many services within a community framework and help promote continuity. Mary Welsh, the Early Years Development Officer, is keen to build on the opportunities which already exist and develop models of good integrated practice which can lead the way.

Roy Earnshaw, Education Officer for SEN, also shares the authority's vision:

> We don't want parents to feel they have to fight a battle – or be passed on from one department to the next. Most of us are in the job because we have the interests of children at heart. We are trying to work together to support families and trust must start from when a child's needs are first identified. We must have the courage to invest in children as early as possible. Rather than an over emphasis on writing Statements we need to focus the resources we have on working in partnership with all sections of the community and neighbourhood schools to meet children's needs. Although flexible and responsive provision is required, we also need a strong commitment within the local community to all of its children. It is important that the school a child goes to has an investment in that child.

Resources

Meeting SEN is expensive. The amount of money available and what it is spent on are of central importance. The answer does not, however, lie in fudging the resources issue. Honesty and clear thinking about the entire SEN budget, criteria about resource allocation and overt priorities give a rationale to decisions. This should promote equal opportunities. The alternative is that whoever shouts loudest wins the resources lottery.

There are no simple answers, but it may be useful to consider the following:

- the more transparency there is about resources, the more accountable people will be for how they are spent. This applies to LEAs and to individual schools and nurseries.
- central joint planning is likely to make better use of existing resources
- the more creative and flexible policy makers and budget holders are, the better use they will be able to make of existing resources
- where joint planning takes a longer-term view, less resources will be required to fund expensive crisis intervention
- where local authorities explore the possibilities for regional collaboration, specialised provision will remain viable and potentially less expensive than other options
- the more joint structures there are, the less need there will be for expensive one-off decision making meetings
- the more emphasis there is on collaborative early intervention, the better the outcomes for individual children – and the more cost effective
- where resources are allocated to developing partnership with parents, the greater understanding there will be about needs, expectations and interventions. This empowers parents to be more effective.
- where the promotion of effective channels of communication is a priority both in and out of school, the more effective each professional and each service will be
- the less duplication there is, the less waste or resources there will be
- the more emphasis that is put on working together, the more supported individuals will feel
- the more supported individuals feel, the more able they will be to meet children's needs.

Time

> Good communication takes time. Services under pressure find that this is often the easiest place to make savings. It may be the most costly. (Ball 1998)

Time issues bridge the organisational and interpersonal levels of working together. Developing relationships, getting to know and understand each other's working practices, clarifying joint objectives and ironing out misunderstandings takes time, at least initially. Making sure that parents do not feel they are being a 'nuisance' means taking the time to listen. Finding out about a child's needs properly does not happen overnight. When personnel are in short supply but the demands of the job increase incrementally, time becomes the most precious resource of all.

Services that experience staff cuts year on year but are expected to carry the same workload will inevitably be less effective. In such situations time priorities need to be renegotiated with senior managers and then communicated to service users.

Time is finite. Demands are not. Priorities need to be made. When initial planning does not happen, time is spent re-inventing the wheel, repeating the same information to different people, having impromptu crisis intervention meetings and generally not putting valuable time to the

Planning ahead or...   Crisis management – today
                                        tomorrow... and next week

best use. Meetings that are planned well in advance so that everyone can prepare for them are likely to be more effective. When information is kept where everyone knows how to get at it quickly no one has to spend hours in futile searches. When support systems are set up so that everyone knows when other people are available, less time is taken up in chasing individuals. When inter-agency work is seen as productive, practitioners make their attendance at joint meetings a priority. This may save time and effort in trying to make contact with elusive colleagues.

Maybe the real world is not so tidy as this – but there needs to be a will to spend time in planning. There is little point in having a stressed and less effective workforce because the time has not been spent on planning how to use it most effectively. This applies both to the service managers, their expectations of their workforce and the priority they genuinely put on collaborative practices to the day-to-day planning of those who are in regular contact with the child and his family.

Interpersonal issues

Much of the good collaboration that presently takes place all over the country happens where mutually supportive relationships between people are flourishing. Even when structures to promote inter-agency work are in place, these will not thrive unless there is an understanding, trust and value put upon the individual knowledge, skills and approaches of all the collaborative partners. This is not easy to achieve when there are stereotypes, assumptions, professional jealousies and protectionism. Value systems, philosophies, attitudes, expectations and even the language people use all contribute to the success or otherwise of working together. The more people know and understand about each other the more they may be able to look for ways in which they can share the same objectives and focus on these rather than their differences.

Equality

Partnerships are more likely to be successful when there is a balance of power and authority. If one partner is conscious that he has more status or another convinced that her views are right because she has more experience, then any attempt at partnership is immediately undermined.

- Collaboration is not talking to other people. It is doing things together.
- Sharing decisions is not checking out your decisions with someone else. It is making them together.

- Communication is listening as well as talking.
- Equality is everyone taking responsibility for both the problem-definition and the solutions.

This may be particularly difficult where there is a hierarchy or structural power base within the partnership. It is possible, however, to put seniority to one side in order to have a team approach for specific pieces of work. If anyone is to be a true collaborative partner, they must not be in a position where there is a conditional clause to their involvement. This is especially true of parents, e.g. 'if you do this then we will not exclude your child'.

Differences

It is inevitable that professionals will not always agree – even professionals within the same service can hold disparate views. People who work in the public and voluntary sectors are often passionate about what they do and although their level of commitment is laudable, they may become blinkered to the potential usefulness of other perspectives. Parents may find themselves lost in the debate.

One answer to this is to empower parents to make the decisions for their children. Differing views can be presented to parents with the advantages and disadvantages of each. If arguments for and against are made in a professional and non-emotive way the parent can be left to judge. Parents may be aided in their deliberations by voluntary bodies and parent supporters and it is helpful if they have opportunities to ask questions and, where appropriate, visit provision.

It is hard for people to shift in their thinking but this is what multi-disciplinary work often entails. Working more closely in teams, with the needs of the child as central, may eventually lead to a greater mutual understanding, respect and tolerance of differences.

Confidentiality

Issues of confidentiality may have a significant impact on communication between different agencies and also within schools. Ideally collaborative partners should share the same relevant information but parents do not always want other people to know about their child's difficulties. They fear labelling and negativity and may be embarrassed. This is accentuated when information is about family circumstances, and/or when the information is given to people who work in the school but also have social links with others in the community. Parents need to be central to the decision making process about who in school is told what about the child and the family.

The medical profession has a very strict code of ethics concerning confidentiality and its members are unable to divulge any information at all without express, written parental permission unless to another medical practitioner.

Child and adolescent mental health teams, although not all doctors, are particularly careful about the information they give out – some families do not want anyone to know that their child is seeing a psychiatrist or is having therapy. This is understandable but can be frustrating for others who are working with the child. Sometimes a limited form of information is helpful if the parents are agreeable. This would indicate appropriate approaches for teachers to take with the child or situations to avoid. Such a communication does not betray confidence but makes a sensible contribution to collaborative working.

Essentially information belongs to the family and it should only be shared with their explicit agreement. Some services ask parents to sign a form that gives them permission to communicate with others who work with the child. It is good practice for this to be explained in terms of what will be shared with whom and for what purpose. This would usually be on a 'need to know' basis. Any more sensitive information should be discussed separately. Family violence, for instance, may be contributing significantly to a child's difficulties, but it would be better for the parent to decide for herself which people she feels comfortable knowing about the situation. This is likely to depend on the trust that is built up, how safe it feels to talk and the difference it is perceived it might make for the child.

Lack of information, however, can be damaging. When people do not know the facts they may be tempted to make assumptions or fall into judging by stereotypes. The case study given here is an illustration of this.

Case study

Karen, a behaviour support teacher, was asked to work with Peter, a young boy with hydrocephalus. Her assessment of the situation provided some interesting and useful insight:

Peter was considered to be aggressive by the teaching staff, not only because of incidents in the playground but also because of assumptions regarding his condition. The only information that staff had received was via informal discussion with Peter's mother. She did not want her child 'labelled' and therefore had actively resisted any school contact with health professionals. Staff were under the impression that a child with hydrocephalus would inevitably be aggressive.

Following the concern that the school were expressing about incidents in the playground she finally agreed to go ahead with a multidisciplinary meeting. The professionals who attended were able to dispel the perception that hydrocephalus and aggression were inextricably linked. Karen's assessment also pointed to other reasons for the rise in incidents in the playground.

This additional information gave staff a fresh perspective and understanding. Interventions were planned for group work on 'safe playground behaviour', and extending play opportunities. This improved the situation for everyone.

Joint training

One way of developing collaborative practice is multi-agency professional development. This could be:

- sessions taken together with outside speakers
- sessions in which professionals describe their practices to others
- joint delivery on specific topics.

Training could be given by parents and professionals on their perspectives of an aspect of SEN, by teachers and professionals presenting together or by any combination of different agencies. Giving participants opportunities to discuss and problem solve with each other in mixed groups is more likely to foster mutual understanding than relying solely on presentations.

Summary

'Working together can be wonderful when everyone pulls together.' This quote from a professional working with early years children and their families sums up both the difficulties and the rationale for collaboration.

This chapter has summarised some of the many and complex issues that may be involved in 'pulling together' but, whatever the challenges, we must continue to strive for ever more collegiate practices. For when we are successful, families are empowered and supported, professionals feel more valued and have greater job satisfaction and, most importantly, children are more likely to have an optimum learning experience.

APPENDIX 1

Information and resources on Special Educational Needs

General information and advice on SEN

Advisory Centre for Education (ACE)
Unit 1B Aberdeen Studios
22–24 Highbury Grove
London N5 2DQ
☎ 020 7354 8321 advice line
afternoons

National Association for Special
Educational Needs (NASEN)
Nasen House
4–5 Amber Business Village
Amber Close
Amington
Tamworth
Staffordshire B77 4RP
☎ 01827 311500

Invalid Children's Aid Nationwide
(ICAN)
Barbican City Gate
1–3 Dufferin Street
London EC1Y 8NA
☎ 020 7374 4422

Council for Disabled Children
8 Wakley Street
London EC1V 7QE
☎ 020 7843 6058

Organisations which promote the inclusion of children with SEN in mainstream education

Centre for Studies on Inclusive
Education (CSIE)
1 Redland Close
Elm Lane
Bristol BS6 6UE
☎ 0117 923 8450

Integration Alliance
Unit 2, Ground Floor
70 Lambeth Road
London SW8 1RL
☎ 020 7735 5277

Parents for Inclusion
Address as above
☎ Office: 020 7735 7735
☎ Help Line: 020 7582 5008

The Alliance for Inclusive Education
Unit 2, Ground Floor
70 South Lambeth Road
London SW8 1RL
☎ 020 7735 5277

Early years organisations

Early Childhood Unit
National Children's Bureau
8 Wakley Street
London EC1V 7QE
☎ 020 7843 6000

National Early Years Network
77 Holloway Road
London N7 8JZ
☎ 020 7607 9573

British Association for Early
Childhood Education (BAECE)
111 City View House
463 Bethnal Green Road
London E2 9QY
☎ 020 7739 7594

Legal advice

Children's Legal Centre
University of Essex
Wivenhoe Park
Colchester
Essex CO4 3SQ
☎ 01206 873820

National Youth Advocacy Service
1 Downham Road South
Heswall
Wirral
Merseyside L60 5RG
☎ Office 0151 342 7852
☎ 0800 616 101

Law Society Children Panel
The Law Society
113 Chancery Lane
London WC2A 1PL
☎ 020 7242 1222 ext. 3286 and 3308

The Advocacy Unit
The Children's Society
14 Cathedral Road
Cardiff, CF1 9LJ
☎ 01222 668956

Children's Rights Office
319 City Road
London EC1V 1LJ
☎ 020 7278 8222

Parent support

Contact a Family
170 Tottenham Court Road
London W1P OHA
☎ 020 7383 3555
(among other things provides support to parents and professionals who are setting up and running groups – see website on
http//www.cafamily.org.uk)

Independent Panel for Special
Educational Advice (IPSEA)
4 Ancient House Mews
Woodbridge
Suffolk 1P12 1DH
☎ 01394 38281
☎ 0800 018 4016

Network 81
1–7 Woodfield Terrace
Stanstead
Essex CM24 8AJ
☎ Helpline 01279 647415
(for parents whose children are having a statutory assessment of their special educational needs)

Voluntary organisations concerned with specific SEN

British Allergy Foundation
Deepdene House
30 Belgrove Road
Welling
Kent DA16 3PY
☎ 020 8303 8525

The National Asthma Campaign
Providence House, Providence Place
London N1 0NT
☎ Office 020 7226 2260
☎ Helpline 0846 701 0203

National Autistic Society
Willesden Lane
London NW2 5RB
☎ Office 020 7833 2299
☎ Helpline 020 7903 3555

Royal National Institute for the Blind
(RNIB)
224 Great Portland Street

London W1N 6AA
☎ Office 020 7388 1266
☎ Helpline 0345 669999

Association for Brain Damaged
Children
Clifton House
3 St Paul's Road
Foleshill
Coventry CV6 5DE
☎ 01203 665450

Brittle Bones Society
30 Guthrie Street
Dundee DD1 5BS
☎ 01382 204446/204447

Cancer and Leukaemia in Children
Trust
12–13 King Square
Bristol BS2 8JH
☎ 0117 924 8844

Scope (Cerebral Palsy)
6 Market Road
London N7 9PW
☎ Office 020 7619 7100
☎ Helpline 0800 626216

Cystic Fibrosis Trust
11 London Road
Bromley
Kent BR1 1BY
☎ 020 8464 7211

National Deaf Children's Society
15 Dufferin Street
London EC1Y 8PD
☎ Helpline 020 7250 0123

British Diabetic Association
10 Queen Anne Street
London W1M 0BD
☎ 020 7323 1531
☎ Helpline 020 7636 6112

Down's Syndrome Association
155 Mitcham Road
London SW17 9PG
☎ 020 8682 4001

British Dyslexia Association
98 London Road
Reading
Berkshire RG1 5AU
☎ 0118 966 2677
☎ Helpline 0118 966 8271

Dyspraxia Foundation
8 West Alley
Hitchin
Herts SG5 1EG
☎ Helpline 01462 454986

British Epilepsy Association
Anstey House
40 Hanover Square
Leeds LS3 1BE
☎ 0113 243 9393
☎ Helpline 0800 309030

National Eczema Society
163 Eversholt Street
London NW1 1BU
☎ 020 7388 4097

Royal Society for Mentally Handicapped Children and Adults (MENCAP)
123 Golden Lane
London EC1Y 0RT
☎ 020 7454 0454

Association for All Speech Impaired
Children (AFASIC)
347 Central Markets
London EC1A 9NH
☎ Helpline 020 7236 3632

Syndromes without a Name (SWAN)
Support Group for Undiagnosed
Children
16 Achilles Close
Great Wyrley
Walsall,
West Midlands WS6 6JW
☎ 01922 701234

Professional organisations

The Community Practitioners and
Health Visitors Association
50 Southwark Street
London SE1 1UN
☎ 020 7717 4000

The Royal College of Speech and
Language Therapists
7 Bath Place
Rivington Street
London EC2A 3DR
☎ 020 7613 3855

The Chartered Society of
Physiotherapy
4 Bedford Row
London WC1R 4ED
☎ 020 7242 1941

The National Association of Paediatric
Occupational Therapists
Barton's Cottage
Wilmslow
Cheshire SK9 2LL
Fax 01625 530680

The National Portage Association
127 Monksdale
Yeovil
Somerset, BA21 3JE
☎ 01935 471641

The Association of Educational
Psychologists
3 Sunderland Road
Durham DH1 2LH
☎ 0191 384 9512

The British Psychological Society
48 Princess Road East
Leicester LE1 7DR
☎ 01162 549568

British Association of Teachers of
the Deaf
Paul A. Simpson
41 The Orchard
Leven
Beverley
East Yorkshire HU17 5QA
☎ 01964 544243
http://www.rmplc.co.uk/orgs/batod

British Association of Social Workers
16 Kent Street
Birmingham B5 6RD
☎ 0121 622 3911

APPENDIX 2

Useful early years Special Educational Needs resource material

ACE Special Education Handbook

Challen, M. and Majors, K. (1997) *Learning to Support: A Training Course for Special Support Assistants*. Clifton, Bristol: Lucky Duck Publishing. This contains useful checklists.

Save the Children. *Working with Under Eights*. Leaflets, books and training resources on a range of issues for young children, including those with SEN. For a brochure and order form contact:
Save the Children
17 Grove Lane
London SE5 8RD
☎ 020 7703 5400

Hannah Mortimer (1997) *Music Makers*. This provides inclusive activities for children with special needs in pre-school. Available from the author at:
Pill Rigg
Sowerby Under Cotliffe
Northallerton
North Yorkshire DL6 3RH
Activities are cross-referenced to Desirable Outcomes.

Also available from the same author:
Playladders: a checklist of play for children with SEN in mainstream nursery
Starting Out: talking with young children who have special needs about starting school.

Judy Miller (1996) *Never Too Young*. National Early Years Network and Save the Children.
This is a handbook for early years workers on how young children can be involved in decision making.

Challen, M. *My Achievement Record: A Developmental Curriculum*. For early years staff working with children who are developmentally delayed. It provides both a checklist and guidelines for next steps. Available from:

Ms M. Challen
Barking and Dagenham Educational Psychology Service
Seabrook House
22 Shipton Close
Dagenham
Essex RM8 3QR

Sheila Wolfendale *All about Me.* This booklet, now in its second edition, is designed
to build a profile of a child in conjunction with parents. Available from:
NES Arnold
Ludlow Hill Road
West Bridgford
Nottingham NG2 6HD
☎ 0115 971 7700 Free Fax: 0500 410420

The Writers' Press publishes a number of books for young children about a range
of special educational needs. Available from:
The Writers' Press
2309 Mountain View Drive
Suite 190
Boise
Idaho 83706
USA
http://www.writerspress.com/homepage.html

Magination Press is linked to the American Psychological Association. It
specialises in books that help young children deal with personal or
psychological concerns, including a variety of special needs. Many are useful for
promoting inclusive and supportive practices in nurseries and infant schools.
Catalogues can be obtained from:
The Eurospan Group
3 Henrietta Street
Covent Garden
London WC2E 8LU
☎ 020 7240 0856 Fax: 020 7379 0609

APPENDIX 3

Glossary

AFASIC Association for All Speech Impaired Children
CDC   Child Development Centre (sometimes Unit)
CMO   Clinical Medical Officer
COP   Code of Practice for Special Educational Needs
DfEE   Department for Education and Employment
DLA   Disability Living Allowance
DoH   Department of Health
EP   Educational Psychologist
ESW   Educational Social Worker (also known as Educational Welfare Officer)
GP   General Practitioner (Family Doctor)
HI   Hearing Impairment
IEP   Individual Education Plan
LEA   Local Education Authority
MO   Medical Officer
NCVO   National Council for Voluntary Organisations
OFSTED Office for Standards in Education
OT   Occupational Therapist
QCA   Qualifications and Curriculum Authority
RNIB   Royal National Institute for the Blind
SEN   Special Educational Needs
SENCO   Special Educational Needs Coordinator
SLT   Speech and Language Therapist
SOEID   Scottish Office Education and Industry Department
SSD   Social Services Department
VI   Visual Impairment

Bibliography

Ball, M. (1998) *Disabled Children: Directions for their Future Care*. Wetherby, Yorkshire: Social Care Group Department of Health and the Council for Disabled Children.

Barnado's (1996) *What Works: Effective Interventions for Children and their Families in Health, Social Welfare, Education and Child Protection*. Ilford: Barnado's.

Cullen, K. (1995) *Multi-professional collaboration? An investigative case study with particular reference to a local authority pre-school home visiting service to families of children with Special Educational Needs*. Unpublished M.Sc. thesis. London: Institute of Education.

Daly, B. and Miller, S. (eds) (1993) *Portage – Providing Quality Services*. Yeovil, Somerset: National Portage Association.

DfE (1994) *Code of Practice on the Identification and Assessment of Special Educational Needs*. London: Central Office of Information.

DfEE (1997a) *Excellence for All Children: Meeting Special Educational Needs* (Green Paper). London: The Stationery Office.

DfEE (1997b) *The SENCO Guide*. London: The Stationery Office.

DfEE (1998a) *Excellence for All: Meeting Special Educational Needs: A Programme of Action*. London: The Stationery Office.

DfEE (1998b) *Early Years Development and Childcare Partnership: Planning Guidance 1999–2000*. London: The Stationery Office.

Department of Health (1991) *The Children Act 1989: Guidance and Regulations; Volume 6, Children with Disabilities*. London: HMSO.

Dickins, M. (1998) 'Forging an Alliance'. *Coordinate 67*. London: The National Early Years Network.

Dyson, A., Lin, M. and Millword, A. (1998) *Effective Communication Between Schools, LEAs and Health and Social Services in the Field of SEN*. Newcastle upon Tyne: Special Needs Resource Centre, Department of Education. Also available from Suffolk: DfEE Publications.

Goodinge, S. (1998) *Removing Barriers for Disabled Children: Inspection of Services to Disabled Children and Their Families*. Wetherby, Yorkshire: Social Care Group Department of Health.

Gunner, A. (1997) *The Children (Scotland) Act 1995: Highlight No. 152*. London: National Children's Bureau.

HM Treasury (1998) 'Cross-departmental review of provision for young children', *Comprehensive Spending Review, Chapter 21*. London: The Treasury Office.

Herbert, E. (1994) 'Becoming a special family', in David, T. (ed.) *Working Together for Young Children: Multi-professionalism in Action.* London: Routledge.

Hobson, K. (1997) 'Educational psychologists and inter-agency collaboration for pre-school children', in Wolfendale, S. (ed.) *Meeting Special Needs in the Early Years*, 147–160. London: David Fulton Publishers.

Jones, A. and Bilton, J. (1994) *The Future Shape of Children's Services.* London: National Children's Bureau.

Makins, V. (1997) *Not Just a Nursery... Multi-agency Early Years Centres in Action.* London: National Children's Bureau.

Mooney, A. and Munton, A. G. (1997) *Research and Policy in Early Childhood Services: Time for a New Agenda.* London: Institute of Education.

Mortimer, H. (1997) 'Surveying professional practice in the early years: multi-disciplinary assessment teams', in Wolfendale, S. (ed.) *Meeting Special Needs in the Early Years*, 136–146. London: David Fulton Publishers.

North Yorkshire County Council: Pupil and Parent Services (1998) *Desirable Learning for All: Implementing the Code of Practice in Pre-Schools and Nurseries.* Northallerton: North Yorkshire County Council.

OFSTED (1998) *Are You Ready for your Inspection? A Guide for Nursery Education Providers in the Private, Voluntary and Independent Sectors.* Suffolk: DfEE Publications.

Payne, L. (1998) *Standards and Frameworks Act 1998: Highlights No. 162.* London: National Children's Bureau.

QCA (1998) *An Introduction to Curriculum Planning for Under Fives.* Hayes, Middlesex: QCA Publications.

Roffey, S. and O'Reirdan, T. (1997) *Infant Classroom Behaviour: Needs, Perspectives and Strategies.* London: David Fulton Publishers.

Rogers, W. S. and Roche, J. (1991) *The Children Act 1989: A Guide for the Education Service.* Milton Keynes: Open University Press.

Sammons, P. *et al.* (1995) *Key Characteristics of Effective Schools: a Review of School Effectiveness Research.* London: OFSTED.

Sebba, J. and Sachdev, D. (1997) *What Works in Inclusive Education?* Ilford: Barnado's.

SOEID (1994) *Effective Provision for Special Educational Needs* (EPSEN). Edinburgh: SOEID.

SOEID (1996) *Children and Young Persons with Special Educational Need: Assessment and Recording.* Circular 4/96. Edinburgh: SOEID.

Stobbs, P. (1998) 'A meaningful partnership', *Coordinate* **68**. London: The National Early Years Network.

Stoll, L. and Fink, D. (1997) *Changing our Schools: Linking School Effectiveness and School Improvement.* Buckingham: Open University Press.

Turner, S. *et al.* (1998) 'Supporting families with deaf children under five:policy, practice and collaboration between Education and Social Services Departments', *British Journal of Special Education* **25**(1), 33–40.

Wilson, R. A. (1998) *Special Education in the Early Years.* London: Routledge.

Wolfendale, S. (1997) 'The state and status of Special Educational Needs in the early years' in Wolfendale, S. (ed.) *Meeting Special Needs in the Early Years*, 1–13. London: David Fulton Publishers.

Wolfendale, S. and Cook, G. (1997) *Evaluation of Special Educational Needs Parent Partnership Schemes.* Suffolk: DfEE Publications.

Index